# INVEST

## LIKE A

# FOX...

## NOT LIKE A

# HEDGEHOG

# INVEST
## LIKE A
# FOX...
## NOT LIKE A
# HEDGEHOG

How You Can Earn
Higher Returns

ROBERT C. CARLSON

John Wiley & Sons, Inc.

Published by John Wiley & Sons, Inc., Hoboken, New Jersey.
Published simultaneously in Canada.

Wiley Bicentennial Logo: Richard J. Pacifico.

For general information on our other products and services or for technical support, please contact our Customer Care Department within the United States at (800) 762–2974, outside the United States at (317) 572–3993 or fax (317) 572–4002.

Wiley also publishes its books in a variety of electronic formats. Some content that appears in print may not be available in electronic formats. For more information about Wiley products, visit our Web site at www.wiley.com.

*Library of Congress Cataloging-in-Publication Data*

Carlson, Robert C., 1957-
    Invest like a fox, not like a hedgehog : how you can earn higher returns
with less risk / Robert C. Carlson.
        p. cm.
    ISBN 978-0-470-12633-2 (cloth)
    1. Investments.   2. Risk management.   3. Investment analysis.   I. Title.
    HG4521.C2685 2007
    332.6–dc22                                                   2007005016

Printed in the United States of America

10   9   8   7   6   5   4   3   2   1

*To my colleagues on the Boards of Trustees
and the staff, past and present, of the
Fairfax County Employees' Retirement
System and the Virginia Retirement System*

# Contents

# Foreword

Institutional investment portfolios—from pension funds to endowments and foundations—are undergoing massive changes as their managers deal with the rapidly changing investment world. This dramatic evolution came into focus with the stock market collapse of 2000 to 2002 and the simultaneous plunge in interest rates engineered by the Federal Reserve from late 2000 through early 2004. The bear market in equities highlighted the extreme concentration of most portfolios in the single-risk factor of the stock market, meaning that the asset pool was primarily dependent on one asset. While the value of portfolios was declining, the drop in interest rates generated an explosion of the discounted value of the liabilities those assets are required to support. Instead of having the luxury of counting on "stocks for the long haul," fund sponsors realized that effective fund management was a function of both asset performance and liability management. Poor execution of either of those responsibilities could create a funding crisis for the governments, corporations, and other entities that support the programs.

The realization that the traditional asset management activities of institutional portfolios left the funds highly exposed to the single risk factor of the stock market created the need for their managers to be more intelligent about risk allocation. The managers also realized that more than just traditional diversification was needed, since the addition of the typical bond portfolio reduces risk but also reduces returns to an extent that the fund cannot achieve required targets. Instead, portfolio managers need a proactive approach to risk management and asset structuring that had never been considered previously.

Fortunately, the financial marketplace has simultaneously evolved. Over the last 10 years, there has been an explosion of investment vehicles, asset overlay techniques, and implementation strategies that revolutionize the ability of managers to implement their strategic and tactical investment goals. At the most basic level, these tools allow managers to segregate and isolate specific return streams into their component parts and thus manage those returns independently. For example, in the past a fund might have hired an International Equity manager to provide exposure to developed market stocks. This decision gave the fund: (1) international stock market exposure (beta); (2) foreign currency exposure (a different beta); and (3) the manager's skill in selecting stocks that outperform those exposures (alpha). Now the tools exist so the fund sponsor can isolate the stock manager's alpha, separately size and manage the international equity exposure, and perhaps neutralize the currency exposure. This ability to focus on the specific return drivers enhances portfolio efficiency and the amount of return that can be earned relative to the risk taken. Also, the stock manager will be able to enhance his or her performance by removing the constraints of the old portfolio structure. The manager might be freed to both buy his or her best ideas for earning above-market returns and to sell short the assets he or she is most confident will underperform. Since the strongest opinion may be what *not* to own, this could significantly improve alpha.

Yet in spite of the newly apparent needs to modify portfolio goals and the greatly expanded tool set available to apply to that task, something is missing from the traditional management of portfolios. That element is the dynamic thinking necessary to change from the traditional path. The willingness to be different from one's peers; to seek excellence even if the result isn't apparent in the short run; the recognition that the primary goal is absolute returns not returns relative to somebody else; the freedom of thought to embrace formerly forbidden tools such as leverage, shorting, and derivatives are what separate dynamic thinking from the static mind-set. This adaptive, flexible approach is what produces results in the next era of investments—and Bob Carlson clearly defines and explains this different approach as thinking like a fox, avoiding the hedgehog mentality.

Bob Carlson is a visionary thought leader who brings years of experience and leadership to the implementation of this dynamic process. As the Chairman of the Board of Trustees of the Fairfax County Employees' Retirement System, Bob not only promoted this new way of thinking, but was instrumental in introducing, building, and implementing that thought process into the investment programs for the plan. As a staff member whom Bob recruited, I was given the responsibility for strategy and implementation. I was constantly encouraged to think dynamically about introducing new programs, converting to portable alpha concepts and implementing a dramatically different asset allocation program. These programs put the plan into the forefront of government pension fund management and top decile performance. In Bob's terms, we acted like foxes, not hedgehogs. In this book, Bob translates the new institutional investment thinking into terms and strategies for individual investors. He has consolidated many of these flexible and dynamic processes into clear and usable directions to assist both institutional and individual investors alike.

Thomas H. Weaver, CFA
Managing Director
FrontPoint Partners
Morgan Stanley Investment Management

# Preface

Why do investors earn lower returns than they should? There is consensus that most investors earn unsatisfactory returns, a conclusion that is supported by anecdotes, casual observations, and research studies.

I know an investment manager of about four-decades experience who routinely asks potential new clients about their past investment experiences. From their response, he estimated that during the great bull market of the 1980s and 1990s most of these investors earned about 7 percent annually compared with a strong double-digit annualized return from the S&P 500. The 7 percent return is probably a high estimate since most investors remember their investment successes but have trouble recalling their losses.

Other information suggests that a 7-percent-annualized return would be a step up for most individual investors. Various studies conducted over the years conclude that most investors earn less than 7 percent annually even in good markets.

Morningstar, the mutual fund and stock-rating and research service, holds an annual conference geared primarily to professional investment advisers. One of the recurring themes of presentations at this conference is that mutual fund investors earn lower returns than the funds themselves. The lower returns occur primarily because the investors buy and sell too often—and often at the wrong times. A significant percentage of individual investors tend to sell investments near their low prices and buy near their high prices, the exact opposite of successful investing. The majority of investors would earn higher returns if they simply held their initial investment positions.

An annual study published by Dalbar Inc., a mutual fund research firm, consistently shows investors in equity mutual funds earning less than the S&P 500 and bond fund investors earning less than a major bond market index. The Dalbar study simply tracks monthly flows in and out of mutual funds and uses the flows to estimate what the investors earned compared to simply holding an index fund. One can question the methodology of the Dalbar studies and the precision of their estimated returns for investors. But the studies do give a good general picture of investor behavior. It is difficult to refute the conclusion that during most time periods individual investors are making mistakes and earning lower returns than they could have.

Studies of 401(k) plans also reveal disappointing results for many investors. In the aggregate, 401(k) investors make such mistakes as putting too much money in either low-returning investments or the sponsoring company's stock. Younger investors tend to be too conservative or risk-averse. Since time is on their side, it would be to their advantage to invest a high percentage of their portfolios in higher-risk, higher-returning investments such as stocks. Most of them do not. Older investors, trying to make up for lost time, tend to take more risk than might be appropriate for them. Investors in 401(k) plans also tend to change their portfolio allocations too frequently and often at the wrong time.

Individual investors are not the only ones reaping lower returns than they could. Many institutional investors—such as mutual funds and pension plans—frequently earn less than their targets and goals.

# A DOG OF A STRATEGY

The history of the Dogs of the Dow investment strategy is a good example of why investors earn lower returns than they should.

The Dogs of the Dow—derived from sorting and manipulating years of market data—has everything investors want in a strategy. It is simple, low cost, and requires little work. Best of all, it produced superior returns as documented by decades of market history.

Under the Dogs of the Dow strategy, the investor ranks by dividend yield the 30 stocks in the Dow Jones Industrial Average and buys the 10 stocks with the highest yields. Usually a dividend yield is high because the stock price has declined. The stocks with the highest yields usually have declined the most in the recent past, hence the name *Dogs of the Dow*. One year later, the exercise is repeated. Stocks that no longer are in the highest yielding 10 are replaced with stocks that have entered the group. The investor needs to act only once a year.

The strategy had been discussed for years but gained popularity in 1991 when its historic success was documented by Michael O'Higgins in *Beating the Dow: A High-Return, Low-Risk Strategy for Outperforming the Pros Even When Stocks Go South* (New York: HarperCollins, 2000). The success was hypothetical because the documentation showed the results that would have been achieved if an investor had followed the strategy. Subsequently, numerous articles appeared praising the book and the strategy. Other books over the next few years also touted the Dogs of the Dow strategy, sometimes giving it a different name to make the strategy appear to be unique to the new book. Finally, mutual funds and unit investment trusts were formed to follow the strategy (though one of the appeals of the strategy is that it is easy and inexpensive to follow; fees paid to investment managers are not necessary). *Barron's* had an annual feature updating how the strategy fared over the past year and listing the stocks an investor should own to follow the strategy for the next 12 months. Some books and articles modified the original strategy to either make it simpler or boost returns or both.

Suddenly, the Dogs of the Dow stopped delivering excess returns. The returns from buying the highest-yielding stocks in the Dow no longer consistently topped the return of the Dow itself. The strategy's popularity quickly faded. The mutual funds implementing it disappeared or shrank in size, and the media coverage dissipated.

This is but one example of an oft-repeated cycle of events in the investment world. An investment or a strategy earns above-average returns and captures the attention of the media and of investors. Money flows into the strategy. Quickly and without warning the excess returns from the strategy or investment fade. The attention of the media and investors, along with investment capital, shifts elsewhere.

Actions that lead to disappointing investment returns can be placed in two categories. There are strategies, or macro-actions, and tactics, or micro-actions. The Dogs of the Dow is a strategy. For most investors, the strategy selected has a much greater influence on investment returns than tactics do. The strategy also indicates whether an investor is more like a fox or a hedgehog. Most of this book will discuss investment strategies. In Chapter 7, and at different points in other chapters, tactics will be discussed because they do affect returns. But strategies are the focus of the book and should be the focus of most investors.

## THE BUG VS. THE WINDSHIELD

A popular song in the 1990s observed that on some days we are like a windshield, and on other days we are more like a bug. It is similar to the saying that some days you eat the bear, and some days the bear eats you. Successful investors have a similar saying: The first rule of investing is to avoid large losses. In other words, the primary goal of every investor is to minimize the number of days he or she is the bug. Instead of focusing on maximizing returns and potential returns as most investors do, the investor should focus on risks and potential risks.

Consider the experience of Virginia's Fairfax County Employees' Retirement System. I have served on the Board of Trustees of this system since 1992 and have been its Chairman since 1995. In the mid-1990s, the board became concerned that the above-average stock returns earned since 1982 would reverse course at some point. If that were to occur, the portfolio's value would decline, perhaps by a significant amount. That would cause a sharp increase in the amount of money the employer (the county government) would be required to contribute to the plan. More than likely, a stock market decline would occur at the same time as an economic recession, when the county government would be pinched for money because of lower tax revenue.

To avoid these consequences, the board reduced the risk in its portfolio. It reduced the allocation to equities. In addition, the U.S. equity portion of the portfolio was tilted to overweight value stocks instead of trying to track the major indexes. A few other changes were made. The portfolio became different from what it was and also was very different from portfolios of comparable public pension funds.

For the rest of the bull market, the portfolio continued to earn solid returns of between 12 percent and 14 percent annually, exceeding its target return. These returns often trailed the market benchmarks and the returns of portfolios constructed using traditional strategies. Each calendar quarter the fund received a report showing where the fund's returns ranked among those of other public pension funds. The fund consistently ranked between the 50th and 80th percentile, meaning that at least 50 percent of other public pension funds had higher returns. Some funds had significantly higher returns.

The objective, however, was not to earn the highest returns among public pension funds in the short term. The goal was to reduce the risk of substantial losses in a bear market while continuing to meet or exceed the rate of return target of 7.5 percent annually. By avoiding large bear market losses, it was believed the fund would earn higher long-term returns.

Once the bear market began after 1999, the strategy proved successful. The fund's losses were modest compared to those of other funds. In 2000, the fund had a positive return of two percent. In 2001, it lost only 2.63 percent, and in 2002 the portfolio declined only 6.93 percent. In 2003, there was a positive return of 27.88 percent. In the quarterly rankings, the fund consistently ranked in the top quarter of funds after 1999 and often was in the top 10 percent. At the end of 2003, the fund was in the top 6th percentile over three years and the top 14th percentile for five-year returns. Occasionally, it was in the top one percentile of public pension funds for quarterly or annual returns. More importantly, after the bear market ended, the fund returned to its previous high value fairly quickly and was back on the path to reaching new highs before most other funds were.

This is one example of how investment returns are enhanced over the long term by focusing on risk instead of short-term returns and by being willing to use investment strategies that are different from popular strategies.

In this book, we see why widely followed strategies are likely to fail to meet an investor's goals and will incur large losses that reduce long-term returns. We also discover an explanation of investment markets that explains market volatility as well as the long-term bull and bear markets to which most investment assets are subject. This knowledge will help us develop investments strategies that will avoid large losses and meet long-term goals.

We also classify investors as foxes and hedgehogs. How an investor thinks is more likely to influence success than is the selection of a particular investment strategy or tactics. Foxes and hedgehogs think differently. An investor with more foxlike characteristics has a greater chance of avoiding large losses. A hedgehog investor can be successful for a period of time, but over an investment lifetime a hedgehog investor is likely to be disappointed. To be consistently successful, an investor must be more like a fox. The more characteristics of a fox an investor has, the more likely the investor is to earn higher returns than the average hedgehog investor.

In Chapter 1, we learn the difference between hedgehogs and foxes and give examples from the investment and sports worlds. We learn that hedgehogs can be successful investors—but their task is more difficult. The markets work against long-term success for hedgehogs. The chapter explains why investors want to be hedgehogs and the mistakes they typically make.

Chapter 2 details two classic hedgehog strategies. We discover the theory behind the strategies, when they worked, and why they stopped producing positive results for investors. Chapter 3 focuses on the widely used strategy generally known as the Capital Asset Pricing Model. We explore why the strategy has become more controversial in recent years as the bear market of the early 2000s revealed some shortcomings.

In Chapter 4 we encounter a little-known explanation of markets that demonstrates why hedgehog strategies are unlikely to be successful. The explanation builds on traditional market theory to explain why markets are not always efficient and are prone to what I call the valuation cycle. Investors need to incorporate this fact in their strategies. Chapter 5 shows how the theory works by walking through an actual valuation cycle.

In Chapter 6 we learn that even investors who know about the valuation cycle have a tendency to think like hedgehogs when developing their strategies. Acknowledging the valuation cycle is one step in learning to think like a fox. Investors also need the thoughts of the Rev. Thomas Bayes, the British mathematician and Presbyterian minister, as well as information from other fields to develop profitable investment strategies. Armed with the Bayes theorem, we then develop successful strategies.

In Chapter 7, we examine some mistakes commonly made by both foxes and hedgehogs. Often, these are tactical mistakes and were identified and classified by the growing field of behavioral finance.

Finally, in Chapter 8, we forecast what portfolios are likely to look like in the future. Recently developed financial tools allow the investor to overcome many of the disadvantages of traditional portfolios. We learn when it is appropriate to use these tools and how they can control risk, improve diversification, and increase returns. We take a look at how some sophisticated investors are using these tools today and how they are rapidly becoming available to individual investors.

There are a number of strategies that can help an investor achieve his or her goals. Most investors choose the wrong strategy and earn lower returns than they should because of how they think about the markets and their portfolios. In this book, we learn how to think differently about investing and to use that new way of thinking to develop a winning investment strategy.

# Acknowledgments

I have benefited from the experience and wisdom of a number of investment professionals over the years. I would like to acknowledge in particular three who reviewed all or parts of the manuscript and made helpful comments. These are Andrew Spellar of the Fairfax County Retirement Administration Agency, Thomas Weaver, formerly of the Wisconsin Alumni Research Foundation and now with the FrontPoint Partners division of Morgan Stanley, and Daniel Bernstein of Bridgewater Associates, Inc.

# About the Author

Robert C. Carlson is editor of the monthly financial newsletter *Retirement Watch* and the web site www.RetirementWatch.com. Since 1995 he has been Chairman of the Board of Trustees of the Fairfax County Employees' Retirement System, which oversees a $2.5 billion portfolio. He also is managing member of Carlson Wealth Advisors, LLC, and served on the Board of Trustees of the Virginia Retirement System. He is an attorney and has passed the CPA exam. He is author of *The New Rules of Retirement: Strategies for a Secure Future* (Hoboken, NJ: John Wiley & Sons, 2005) and a number of research reports. He has appeared on numerous radio shows and been quoted in publications ranging from the *Wall Street Journal* to *Barron's*, *Money*, the *Washington Post*, and *Reader's Digest*.

# CHAPTER 1

# FOXES VS. HEDGEHOGS

Tiger Woods is a fox. So are Billy Beane and Steven Cohen.
Warren Buffett is mostly a fox, but he has a bit of hedgehog in him.

The investment strategists behind the hedge fund Long-Term Capital Management were full-blooded hedgehogs.

Woods is the best golfer of his generation, and many argue he could end his career as the best golfer ever. Beane is the general manager of the Oakland A's Major League Baseball team. Cohen runs the hedge fund firm SAC Capital Advisors. Buffett is considered one of the most successful investors ever and runs Berkshire Hathaway Inc. (which, among other interests, holds GEICO, the insurance company with the little green gecko).

Long-Term Capital Management was a hedge fund that initially earned investment returns that made others envious but ended in a spectacular, headline-grabbing failure that many speculate could have led to a global financial meltdown were it not for the intervention of federal regulators.

Investors could do very well by emulating the foxlike tendencies of Tiger Woods, Billy Beane, Steven Cohen, and Warren Buffett. Investors are very well advised not to emulate Long-Term Capital Management and other hedgehogs. Investors should strive to be foxes, not hedgehogs. But it is not the specific actions or accomplishments of the foxes named here that should be emulated. Instead, how they think and strategize are the keys to their long-term success. These traits can be learned by others and applied to improve investment returns.

## THE EVOLUTION OF TIGER

Tiger Woods entered the world of professional golf at the top. After winning the amateur title twice, he turned professional and immediately won the first major tournament he entered, the Masters. He not only won the Masters, Woods dominated the tournament and finished 12 strokes ahead of his nearest competitor.

Not long after that victory, however, Woods worked with an instructor to change his swing. That project was productive. In the next seven years, Woods won seven more majors and a host of other tournaments. He often was ranked the top golfer in the world.

At the top of the golf world and seemingly at the top of his game, Woods sought another instructor and again set about changing his swing. As instructor Hank Haney explained to the *Wall Street Journal* ("Struggles at the Top" by John Paul Newport, June 17, 2006), nothing was wrong with Woods's game. But other golfers were responding to his dominance by improving their own games and spending more time in the gym. Woods was among the first professional golfers to make fitness and athleticism important elements of his training program. He could see that other golfers were following this practice and becoming more competitive.

Woods believed that to keep improving and to stay on top, changes had to be made. Woods also was looking forward to the day when he was older and his body not as resilient. The new swing was designed to be more consistent and more powerful, but also to put less strain on the body.

The transition period was a difficult one for Woods. His game slipped, and he did not win any tournaments in 2004. But in 2005 he had perhaps his best year to date, winning six events including two major tournaments. Once again he was the top-ranked golfer in the world, and the successes continued through 2006.

## MONEYBALL PARTS I AND II

Billy Beane gained fame by turning the Oakland A's into a playoff-bound team with a salary budget a fraction of those of perennial powerhouses such as the New York Yankees. Beane, the hero of *Moneyball: The Art of Winning an Unfair Game* by Michael Lewis (New York: W. W. Norton, 2003), located unheralded but quality players by throwing out traditional scouting reports and instead analyzing statistics. A key insight of Beane and his staff was to look beyond traditional statistics such as batting average, home runs, and hits. Instead, they decided that the key statistics were on-base percentage for hitters and the strikeout rate for pitchers. The result was that he found players who performed well in the Major Leagues without having to bid for them against other teams.

Things did not go smoothly for Beane after the publication of *Moneyball*. Other teams began to copy his methods and focus on his key statistics when selecting players. They bid up the prices for players Beane found appealing. Also, the bargain players Beane found in the past became free agents and either signed with or were traded to teams that would pay them more. Compounding these difficulties is that some of the players Beane signed earlier did not reach potential. The A's failed to make the playoffs in 2004 and 2005.

Yet, in 2006, the A's came back to make the playoffs and win their division title before finally losing in the league championship series.

As other teams caught on to his methods, Beane had to change. One move was to analyze the statistics and conclude that a portion of the problem in 2005 was bad luck, not a lack of skilled players. A major reorganization was not required. Two years earlier Beane already had altered his strategy by drafting high school and junior college pitchers. Previously, he drafted primarily four-year college players who had pitched many innings against quality teams. With many other teams now fishing in his pond, Beane moved to another spot. Also, since everyone else was focusing on the on-base percentage of batters, Beane focused on those with the most walks. As for pitchers, since other teams bid up the salaries for pitchers with high strikeout rates, Beane instead sought infielders with good defensive skills to back up the pitchers he could afford.

Beane kept his basic approach of seeking players that were better than the marketplace recognized, and therefore could be had for relatively low salaries. But he changed his way of finding and evaluating value, because other teams were bidding up salaries of players with the qualities he initially sought.


## THE UNKNOWN BILLIONAIRE

Steven Cohen quietly became a billionaire by managing a hedge fund that achieved spectacular returns. From 1992 through 2005, he generated for his investors an average annual return of 43.5 percent, after subtracting his 3 percent annual management fee and 50 percent share of profits.

Cohen earned his high returns by quickly trading in and out of stocks. He often had no knowledge of what a company did or what its financial fundamentals were. Instead, he followed the trading patterns of stocks. He bought and sold based on what was called "tape watching" in the days when stock prices were reported on paper ticker tapes. Investment positions were held for short periods of time (a few weeks on average), and the number of trades was high.

After the bull market ended in 2000, the markets began to change. After 2002, Cohen decided the changes were long term and his strategy needed to adapt. According to a profile published in the *Wall Street Journal* ("The Hedge-Fund King Is Getting Nervous" by Susan Pulliam, September 16, 2006), Cohen altered his strategy to focus more on fundamentals and to hold stocks longer, from 6 to

12 months. He also told investors to expect lower returns in future years because there would be fewer opportunities in the markets. Cohen concluded that the days of making high returns were over as were the days of profiting from quick trading.

## THE FLEXIBLE ORACLE

Warren Buffett was schooled by the legendary Benjamin Graham in the strict value style of investing. Graham's method, explained in detail in *Security Analysis* (New York: McGraw-Hill, 1951) with coauthor David L. Dodd and *The Intelligent Investor* (New York: HarperCollins, 1973, 2003) involves determining the percentage of a firm's value its stock is selling for. Graham preferred using a company's book value and purchasing only stocks that sold for two-thirds or less of the company's book value. Buffett began investing this way and earned strong returns for his investors.

In the late 1960s, Buffett decided that he did not understand the stock market at the time and closed his investment partnership. He returned funds to his investors and began managing a major holding of his portfolio, Berkshire Hathaway. Most of his management involved investing the firm's cash.

Over time, Buffett refined and changed his investment strategy. With guidance from his partner, Charlie Munger, Buffett looked for companies with strong franchises that were selling at reasonable prices. A franchise is a barrier to entry or unique product or service that is difficult for competitors to overcome or imitate. Buffett had another period of spectacular returns by purchasing franchise companies such as local newspapers, Coca-Cola, American Express, and GEICO. Most of the stocks were purchased after bad news caused a price decline. But Buffett has said that the stocks were not purchased solely because they were cheap. The growth potential of their franchises was an essential characteristic a company had to have before it would be purchased.

Buffett again changed his investment approach as the great bull market of the 1990s pushed stock valuations out of his comfort range. This time, Buffett began purchasing entire companies and had them operate as wholly owned subsidiaries of Berkshire Hathaway. Most of the companies were privately held when Berkshire purchased them, and Buffett purchased them in private deals that rarely involved investment bankers. At times, Buffett ventured even further from his original investment strategy. He took a position against the U.S. dollar through futures contracts, and he made his first venture outside the U.S. by purchasing an Israeli company.

Buffett initially gained fame and fortune by purchasing stocks at attractive prices and became known as the Oracle of Omaha. But he changed the details of his investment strategy over time to adapt to changing markets and eventually became the world's second richest person.

## GENIUS CAN FAIL

Long-Term Capital Management was an investment partnership, or hedge fund, formed in March 1994 by some individuals who were prominent in the financial services industry.

LTCM, whose story is told in *When Genius Failed: The Rise and Fall of Long-Term Capital Management* by Roger Lowenstein (New York: Random House, 2000), had a fairly simple strategy, known as *arbitrage*. The basic theory of arbitrage is that prices of assets tend to have historic relationships to each other. For example, high-quality corporate bonds usually offer a higher interest rate than Treasury bonds because of their additional risk. Corporations can go bankrupt, but governments are unlikely to. Except for extreme and short-lived instances, the yield difference is within a certain range. LTCM created databases and computer models that would look for those extreme and short-lived instances when two assets were trading outside of their historic relative value range. After spotting an anomaly, the fund would place investments that would become profitable when the relative values returned to their normal range.

The basic arbitrage strategy would be enhanced in a couple of ways by LTCM. First, LTCM used an extraordinary amount of debt or leverage in its portfolio. Instead of investing only with the money it raised from investors, LTCM would borrow additional money and invest that. This was necessary to increase returns, because the potential profit from most arbitrage opportunities is quite small. To earn a good return on investors' capital, leverage was needed. Most arbitrage operations borrow from 100 percent to 300 percent of their invested capital. LTCM borrowed 10 times and more of its invested capital.

Second, LTCM expanded arbitrage trading into assets that had never before been subject to it. It drifted from the big, liquid market of bonds, usually bonds of governments around the world, into more obscure and less liquid assets for which the history was less reliable and the markets less efficient.

The LTCM strategies were based on a simple premise: Markets are relatively efficient. Inefficiencies appear from time to time. But they are temporary and must soon be corrected. By using computer power and trading models to compute the true value of different investments, LTCM believed it could identify inefficiencies first and buy undervalued assets and sell short overvalued assets before others identified them. Later, it would sell the investments for a profit.

LTCM's first big mistake was not to anticipate competition. While the firm did not disclose its specific trading actions, its general approach to the markets was well known. After all, some of the key partners were professors who had widely published their theories for decades, and the traders at LTCM previously were prominent at other firms.

Once LTCM started to show good results, other Wall Street firms implemented their own variations of the theories. That meant fewer opportunities for LTCM, and the opportunities it did find were less profitable.

LTCM probably made its biggest mistake believing that investing is all science; that there is no art or judgment involved. The firm based its investment positions on computer analyses of market history. The firm concluded that the historic valuation ranges of different assets and the relationships between different assets were normal and would change only for very brief periods. They believed that the markets would not have what the professors referred to as a *10-sigma event*. (Sigma is the Greek letter that statisticians use to represent standard deviation, or volatility. Stock market returns generally fluctuate in a range of two to three standard deviations, or sigmas, from their long-term average return.) They did not believe there were periods when investors became extremely emotional and irrational and remained that way for a while.

Market anomalies, unfortunately, do occur and can persist for a while. Through most of 1998, market conditions were happening that "couldn't happen" according to history. The Russian debt default in the fall of 1998 triggered a market panic, resulting in a 10-sigma event. Even an extreme market anomaly such as that is not a problem if the investor can simply hold on until a reversal eventually comes. It even can be profitable if one has the cash and courage to invest during the panic. But if the investor needs the money that is invested, or if the investments were made with a lot of debt, then the investments must be sold at the worst possible time. In LTCM's case, because of the amount of debt it used to purchase the investments, positions had to be sold after prices fell below certain levels. But buyers could not be found. As Lowenstein wrote, "The professors overlooked the fact that people, traders included, are not always reasonable."

The investment markets failed to follow the rules and models that LTCM had developed. "The mathematicians had not foreseen this. Random markets, they had thought, would lead to standard distributions—to a normal pattern of black sheep and white sheep, heads and tails, and jacks and deuces, not to staggering losses in every trade, day after day after day," wrote Lowenstein. LTCM eventually was bailed out by a consortium of banks put together by the Federal Reserve Bank, and the original partners lost most of their wealth. The lesson learned by one of the key partners whose models had failed was that more elaborate and sophisticated models were needed.

## FOXES AND HEDGEHOGS

The late philosopher Isaiah Berlin wrote an essay, famous in its field, titled "The Hedgehog and the Fox." The essay is an analysis of Russian writer Leo Tolstoy's philosophy of history. The details of the essay are not relevant to investing, but the essay's introduction contains an insight that explains the difference between Tiger Woods, Billy Beane, Warren Buffett, and Steven Cohen on the one hand and Long-Term Capital Management on the other. This insight also describes the difference between many successful investors and investment strategies on the one hand and less successful investors and strategies on the other. The insight points the way to becoming a better investor.

Berlin credits 7th century BCE Greek poet Archilochus with the expression: "The fox knows many things, but the hedgehog knows one big thing." This expression captures, according to Berlin, "one of the deepest differences which divide writers and thinkers, and, it may be, human beings in general."

On one side of the divide are the hedgehogs. These thinkers relate everything to a single vision. They view everything through one central, organizing principle and base everything they understand, think, and feel on that principle. On the other side of the divide are the foxes. They pursue many ends and think and act on many levels. Foxes use a vast variety of experiences and do not try to fit them into one unchanging, all-embracing principle. Or to view it another way, foxes are cunning and eclectic in their thinking and perhaps inconsistent at times. Hedgehogs are dogged, persistent, and very consistent.

Is one way of thinking and making decisions better than the other?

In *Expert Political Judgment: How Good Is It? How Can We Know?* (Princeton: Princeton University Press, 2005), psychologist Philip E. Tetlock tries to identify the better decision-making system. Over several decades, Tetlock and other researchers asked experts to make forecasts. The experts and forecasts generally were related to foreign affairs and international politics. In addition to compiling and determining the accuracy of the forecasts, the researchers also compiled details about the experts. Data was compiled on the backgrounds, philosophies and other characteristics of the experts, including how they thought and made decisions.

The results are counterintuitive. An expert's education, professional background, status, and similar factors did not aid accuracy. The expert's philosophy or core beliefs also did not improve accuracy. In other words, liberals were not more accurate than conservatives; optimists were no better forecasters than pessimists; and realists did not perform better than what Tetlock calls *institutionalists*. None of the factors that most people expect would be clues to a forecaster's accuracy turned out to be useful in identifying the better forecasters.

The key to identifying better forecasters turns out to be Berlin's framework of hedgehogs versus foxes. As Tetlock puts it, "*What* experts think matters far less than *how* they think." The foxes among the surveyed experts turned in more accurate forecasts than the hedgehogs by a sizeable measure. In addition, the long-range forecasts of the foxes were far more accurate than their short-term forecasts and much more accurate than the long-range forecasts of the hedgehogs. The hedgehogs "knew one big thing" and tried to fit new events and a dynamic world into that view. The foxes looked for ad hoc solutions that were consistent with the many little things they knew and that fit the rapidly changing world.

Another factor that helped the foxes is that they were more willing to admit mistakes in prior forecasts and not to make excuses for them. Instead, they would use a point-counterpoint style to analyze what had happened and adapt new forecasts to those observations. The foxes were more self-deprecating. The hedgehogs were more likely to make big mistakes and would build up excessive enthusiasm for their forecasts.

## A Better Way to Think

Tetlock identified six basic ways in which foxes and hedgehogs differed from each other. As we shall see in this book, many of these differences also are likely to separate successful investors from the rest of the pack. The basic differences are:

- Foxes are more skeptical of the usefulness of "covering laws" for explaining the past or predicting the future. Covering laws are those big, central principles that seek to explain many things.
- Foxes are more wary of simple historical analogies.
- Foxes are less likely to get swept away in their own rhetoric.
- Foxes are more worried about our judging those in the past too harshly (and less worried about those in the future judging us harshly for failing to see the obvious).

- Foxes see more value in keeping "political passions under wraps."
- Foxes make more self-conscious efforts to integrate conflicting theories, beliefs, and observations.

Despite the advantages foxes have over hedgehogs, Tetlock did not give them unqualified support. He concluded: "Foxes are not awe-inspiring forecasters: most of them should be happy to tie simple extrapolation models, and none of them can hold a candle to formal statistical models."

It also is worth noting that, of course, not every expert could be classified as either a fox or a hedgehog. There is a linear scale from fox to hedgehog, and many experts fall somewhere along the scale as hybrids of the two rather than as a pure fox or hedgehog. But Tetlock's research found that the closer an expert is to the characteristics of a fox, the better the forecasts were.

We can see how Tiger Woods is a fox.

While at the top of his personal game and his sport, Woods worked hard to make radical changes in his golf swing—twice. He displayed the modesty that Tetlock found is common among foxes. He was regarded as the best, yet he looked for ways to improve. Woods also apparently did not view one aspect of his swing or the golf game as the key to success. Finally, he adapted and changed. Woods realized that his competitors were getting better. In particular, he concluded that to remain at the top he would have to learn to hit longer tee shots. Instead of insisting that the way he played was the right way, Woods took a more objective view and decided on the changes that were needed.

We saw the same pattern from Billy Beane and Steven Cohen. After achieving success with one strategy, each realized that adjustments had to be made. Beane changed the details of his approach, using different criteria to identify quality ball players available at relatively low salaries. Cohen made a bigger adjustment, moving from an investment strategy of quick trading that ignores company fundamentals to one with longer holding periods that analyzes fundamentals.

Warren Buffett likewise changed his investment strategy more than once as the markets changed. At first, he primarily searched for stocks whose prices had been beaten down by market or company events and were cheap. As cheap stocks became less numerous and as he learned more about the markets and investing, Buffett began to search for companies with coveted franchises that he understood and believed were protected. As time went on, Buffett's strategy changed again. He turned his investment vehicle, Berkshire Hathaway, into a major insurance company by acquiring a number of insurers. Also, instead of purchasing portions of publicly traded companies he bought entire companies and owned them as subsidiaries of Berkshire Hathaway.

Yet, there is a bit of a hedgehog in Warren Buffett. At one point in the 1960s he shut down his original investment partnership because he could not find enough stocks that met his investment criteria. Later, throughout the great stock bull market of the 1990s, especially the late 1990s, Buffett's investment returns lagged the market indexes. The bulk of the gains generated by the indexes during that period came from large company growth stocks, especially technology stocks. Buffett maintained that he did not understand technology and would not invest in anything he did not understand. Even his friendship with Bill Gates of Microsoft could not sway Buffett from his stand on technology stocks. While Buffett's steadfast position on technology stocks helped him avoid the worst aspects of the post-1999 market decline, it still excludes a large and fast-growing segment of the economy and stock market from his portfolio.

The managers at Long-Term Capital Management were classic, pure hedgehogs. They established as a lodestar that the investment markets are fairly efficient, and that any inefficiencies would be short-lived. A corollary belief was that past relationships between investments represented efficiency, so price relationships outside the normal range were bound to return to normal. Their theory had no room for changes in investor behavior that would alter historical relationships. Even as events unfolded, they were unwilling to consider the possibility their theory was not working as projected. The strategists learned one big thing and expected all events to fit within that big thing.

## INVEST LIKE A FOX, NOT LIKE A HEDGEHOG

Investment markets are dynamic. They always are changing. An investment market reflects the interactions of millions of humans. People learn over time and adjust their expectations and behavior accordingly. Some aspects of the investment markets are consistent over long periods of time—so far. Over shorter periods, however, long-term relationships often do not hold up. Investors must adapt their investment strategies to capture the dynamism of the investment markets or they will earn lower returns than they should and perhaps suffer large losses. The probability of investment success is greater for foxes than for hedgehogs.

Hedgehogs can be successful investors. But their timing must be right. They must adopt the "one big thing" investment principle at the right time, when that principle is consistent with market trends that are in their early stages. They also must exit the markets at the right time.

Too often, the timing of investment hedgehogs is wrong. They mine the data of investment and economic history to discern patterns and relationships. Then, they develop an investment strategy. That usually is about the time that the dynamism of the markets takes hold. It is a fairly good bet that if there is enough data to discern a pattern or rule for investing, the pattern is about to change and the rule soon will be invalid. (For now, we will skip over the tendency of hedgehogs to draw their rules and conclusions by examining time periods that are too short or that have unique characteristics.)

Investment history is littered with strategies that worked on paper using historical data yet failed to continue working. There is little doubt that most individual investors earn lower returns than they could. Some of the shortfall in returns is due to poor investment discipline. Too many investors chase fads, headlines, and recent past returns. They also trade too often and pay too much in expenses and taxes.

Yet, even many investors who are disciplined and who consistently follow rational strategies earn lower returns than they should, and often that is due to their being hedgehogs. These investors learned "one big thing" about investing and stuck with it. For a while the strategy works, but in time the dynamism of the markets puts their portfolio and its strategy out of sync with investment trends. Many investors are serial hedgehogs. They grasp an investment theory based on one big thing. After a period of poor returns, they discard the theory. But they adopt another strategy based on the next one big thing.

Many hedgehogs adopt their investment strategies because data show the strategy has worked well over a period of time. That might be true, but there are two issues to explore before deciding to follow the strategy to which the data points.

As I have emphasized, markets are dynamic. The aspects of the market that made the strategy so effective in the past might no longer be present. A quick example is the dividend yield on the major U.S. stock indexes. For many years a widely respected and profitable practice among investors was to increase allocations to U.S. stocks whenever the dividend yield exceeded 6 percent or 7 percent. Stocks were considered bargains when the yield was in this range and were likely to earn above-average returns in the following years. The corollary was to reduce stock holdings when the dividend yield fell below 3 percent. This strategy increased returns and reduced risk over many years.

But the markets changed. Investors became less interested in dividends, and many companies chose not to pay dividends. The dividend yield fell below three percent and has remained there. Despite the low dividend yield, the stock indexes rose through the 1980s and 1990s. Anyone who continued to follow the dividend yield strategy missed the best years of the great bull market.

Another issue to explore is how the strategy fares in shorter periods than the very long term. Most of us cannot wait for the long term to make a strategy profitable. Our investment horizons are shorter than that. For example, we might need to accumulate investment capital by retirement age, and then we start to spend the money. Most of us also do not have the patience or fortitude to endure a decade or more of paltry returns without losing faith in a strategy. Many financial and retirement plans simply cannot be successful if investments experience an extended period of below-average returns, regardless of the prospect for long-term returns.

People, especially investors, want to be hedgehogs. They long for simple rules that explain things and that can be used to develop simple approaches to life. This yearning has been true since at least as far back as the Book of Job. As recorded in that book, Job was blameless. God allowed Satan to inflict terrible things on Job to prove his faith. While Job wondered why God would do these things to him, Job's friends insisted that these things could happen to Job only because he and his family had committed great sins. They believed in the simple rule that bad things only happened to people who did bad things. Despite the evidence of Job's blameless life and though they had no evidence of sins committed by Job and his family, they insisted Job must have been a great sinner. We know they were wrong, and later in the book God told them so. Job's friends were classic hedgehogs and clung to simple rules for as long as they could.

The search for simple, universal investment strategies often results in significant losses of capital. Yet, because of the natural inclination to desire such solutions, investors continue to search for hedgehog strategies.

## THE SEARCH FOR PATTERNS

Investment professionals often refer to the search for rules as data mining. Professional and amateur investors alike search historic market and economic data for clues to investment success. Within the data the investors look for patterns—series of events that seem to recur in similar fashions. Sophisticated institutional investors use computers and elaborate mathematics to discern patterns. Investors with fewer resources use a more intuitive process.

Before converting a pattern into an investment rule or strategy, consider some common traps that snare people in this endeavor.

• Random events are easy to confuse with cause and effect. There are numerous actions and events that influence markets and investor behavior. By focusing on a few events and the subsequent market results, a person can conclude that there was a cause and effect or that certain decisions led to certain results.

It is easy to find patterns in what are in fact random events. If a computer is asked to generate randomly a series of one and zeros, at some point patterns would be observed in the output. Perhaps there will be instances of six zeroes preceded by three ones. There is no cause and effect, because the computer is randomly generating the data. But someone simply analyzing the output could see patterns and conclude there is meaning behind them. Likewise, many clever and diligent people have sought to find relationships between the investment markets and Super Bowl results, women's fashion, various cultural trends, and astrology. These efforts are in addition to those that seek to find more rational relationships between investments and interest rates, inflation, or economic growth.

Finding patterns in random events, being "fooled by randomness," is the very subject of Nassim Nicholas Taleb's *Fooled by Randomness: The Hidden Role of Chance in Life and in the Markets* (New York: Texere Thomson, 2004). The book explains how people expect the world, especially the markets, to be linear and predictable. In fact, it is random and unpredictable over any short period.

• Deciding which variables to focus on is another obstacle to those seeking to define an investment strategy. Since investment markets are composed of millions of people making decisions, anything that affects an individual's decision should be considered. No one has the resources to consider all potential variables. So, hedgehogs seeking to discern investment rules must begin by excluding many variables. Yet by excluding variables, the search for patterns is likely to find false patterns and casual relationships.

The variables that affect investment markets are so numerous that using the past to discern the future is an impossible task. The circumstances are different each time, because the variables are too numerous. The situation is never the same as it was in the past.

• An investor must accept that the unexpected, the unlikely, and even the impossible event will occur. Investment markets tend to have what the statisticians call *fat tails* or outliers. Most activities, when graphed, show a normal distribution. In the normal distribution, most results are bunched near the median result. Only a small number of results are far from the median, and that portion of the graph is called the tail. Most graphs have skinny tails with very few results far from the median.

But most investment markets have fat tails in their graphs. A minority of the results is far from the median, but it is a significant minority of events. The frequency of these unlikely events cannot be ignored. For example, some people missed the last few years of the equity bull market of the late 1990s because there never had been a period when the major market indexes increased at least 20 percent each year for more than three consecutive years. Greater than 20 percent gains more than two consecutive years was considered unlikely. Yet, before the bull market was over, the Standard & Poor's 500 Index returned more than 20 percent for each of five consecutive years. Ignoring fat tails is one of the factors that led to the decline of Long-Term Capital Management. Taleb, in *Fooled by Randomness*, refers to such events as *black swans*, an expression for a phenomenon that is out of the common course. Their equivalent occurs in the investment markets with some regularity and investors must be prepared for them.

• The search for patterns in past data is highly dependent on the beginning and ending points used in the search. Numerous researchers have found that conclusions are changed when the time period tested is changed. One reason is that investment markets often have long-term cycles. Changing the time period includes or excludes a significant cycle. Another reason the date is important is one we already have discussed: numerous variables influence the markets. A variable might be dominant in one period but not in another. Still another factor is that public investment markets have existed for only a relatively short period of human history, and they have changed considerably in that time. Even if all available data are used, the time period might not be long enough to be considered statistically significant. If only a portion of the data is used, there likely is not enough data to generate reliable conclusions.

• Once a reliable investment rule is developed, it almost invariably stops working. A prime example is known as the January Effect.

Researchers in the 1970s and 1980s discovered that stocks often produced unusually high returns in January. Further research indicated that the returns were concentrated in the first half of January, especially in small company stocks. The research was published and widely discussed and followed. There even was a book written on the January Effect.

Suddenly, the January Effect stopped working. The reliable above-average returns that could be earned by loading up on small company stocks at the beginning of January disappeared.

This is not an unusual turn of events. Once a pattern is well established it ceases. Perhaps this is because it really was just a random pattern, not something that was going to be repeated. It also is likely that as people learned about the pattern and changed their behavior, the behavioral changes also changed the pattern.

Investment markets are not subject to unchanging laws of nature that are found in physics, engineering, chemistry, and some other fields. Investment markets consist of human beings acting. People tend to learn, change, and adapt over time. They respond differently to what might seem to be the same events each time they occur. And the occurrences never are exactly the same, partly because people are learning and partly because all factors are not exactly the same.

• A final consideration for hedgehogs is that even when a pattern appears, in the investment markets there never is a 100 percent correlation between factors. There might be a high probability that certain occurrences will lead to certain results. But with a probability of less than 100 percent, it rarely is safe to invest an entire portfolio according to the rule. There will be periods when the rule will not work. Though rare, the occurrences could lead to losses high enough to more than offset the gains from the periods when the rule does work. One investment advisor used to say that the best investment rule was to assume that a rule would stop working after you start to use it.

In this book we explore these topics in more detail. In Chapters 2 and 3, we examine some hedgehog strategies investors have been encouraged to follow and that have been widely adopted. We see when they work and when they stop rewarding investors, and we explore why the strategies are not effective over the long term. In Chapter 4, an explanation of the investment markets—their foundation and framework—makes clear why investors need to think like foxes if they hope to be successful in the long term. Chapter 5 takes that framework from theory to practice by using it to explain changes in the U.S. stock markets. Chapter 6 details how to—and how not to—implement an investment strategy for foxes and to think like a fox. In Chapter 7, we discuss some investment mistakes investors are prone to make, whether they are foxes or hedgehogs. Finally, in Chapter 8, we look at new investment tools and how they can enhance the portfolios of investors who think like foxes.

# CHAPTER 2

---

# CLASSIC HEDGEHOG
# INVESTMENT STRATEGIES

I nvestment decisions generally can be divided into two broad types, regardless of whether they are developed by hedgehogs or foxes. There are strategic and there are tactical decisions.

Strategic decisions, or portfolio strategies, are macro or big picture decisions. They focus on the overall allocation of a portfolio between different investments and how those investments interact with each other to determine the portfolio's overall return and other characteristics. Portfolio strategies also set the general rules for when the allocation will be changed and what will determine why the changes are made. Tactical decisions, sometimes referred to as micro or trading decisions, are the decisions to change the allocation of the portfolio. Strategy has a long-term focus, while tactics have a shorter-term focus. The length of the tactical focus depends on the strategy. Some strategies require multiple changes within a day; others require only a few tactical changes each year. Tactical decisions can also include which specific securities, mutual funds, or other investments to buy and sell within an asset class.

Most of the following chapters focus on strategic decisions. Tactical decisions might appear from time to time. But until Chapter 6, strategies are the primary focus. Investors need to get the portfolio strategy right before considering tactical decisions for individual assets.

The rest of this chapter will focus on two classic hedgehog portfolio strategies. Investors will learn when they work, when they do not, when it might be appropriate to use them, and when they are dangerous to one's wealth.

## THE CLASSIC ADVICE

The original hedgehog portfolio strategy is a very simple life-cycle strategy, and it worked well for a number of years.

The strategy is that younger people in the first phase of their investment life should invest primarily for growth. They can afford risk. Time and compound returns will overcome bear markets and other sources of losses. Over time, the percentage of stocks is reduced, and the bonds are increased. *The key part of the strategy is that as one nears retirement, and especially as retirement begins, the portfolio is shifted into safe, income-producing investments.* These investments include annuities, bonds, certificates of deposit, and money market funds. Different advisors have different ideas at which age the shift should be made, how gradual the shift should be, and other mechanics. The strategy ultimately is the same: In retirement, investors should position their portfolios primarily to earn income.

The reasoning behind this advice is simple. A retiree needs regular income to pay expenses, and prefers not to dip into principal to pay for expenses. Principal is preserved as long as possible, preferably to be left to the next generation. Bonds and the other conservative investments pay higher income yields than stocks most of the time and are the appropriate investments for a retiree.

Another consideration is that a retiree or someone near retirement does not want the principal value of the portfolio to fluctuate as much as a growth-oriented portfolio will. A portfolio that is wholly or primarily composed of stocks can decline 20 percent or more in a short period. Even a retiree, who understands that stocks fluctuate in the short term but have high returns over the long term, is often uncomfortable experiencing such a decline in principal. In addition, declines in stock prices can persist for a long time. A secular bear market can last for years. An older investor might not see the portfolio recover during his lifetime.

Bonds and other income-oriented investments tend to be much more stable. They do not have the growth potential of stocks, but they also are very unlikely to lose a substantial percentage of their value. Annuities and certificates of deposit retain their principal value unless the issuing bank or insurer becomes insolvent and the amount invested exceeds the insured amount. Money market funds almost always retain their $1 per share value. Bonds fluctuate with changes in interest rates, but the fluctuations are not as great as those for stocks, and the principal value is restored by holding the bond until maturity unless the issuer defaults.

For those reasons, as investors near retirement they are advised to shift their portfolios to investments that are income-oriented and that maintain a reasonably stable value.

Yet, there are dangers in this classic portfolio strategy. There are times when this strategy is more dangerous than a portfolio of more volatile investments.

## Income Must Grow

The strategy of investing for income in retirement made sense for most retirees at one time. Until fairly recently, life expectancy was much lower. The average retirement lasted about five years. Few people had the 20-, 30-, and 40-year retirements that are becoming common. Some of the problems with income-only investing were manageable within a 5- to 10-year retirement, but they become overwhelming over a longer period.

Also, when the strategy was developed very few retirees depended on their investment portfolios for the bulk of their income. Employer pensions and Social Security provided most retirement income. Individual savings often were supplements to those main sources of retirement income.

Longer retirements and structural changes in the financial markets make this classic hedgehog strategy a poor one for most people who are retired or near retirement.

The most serious problem with long-term income investing is inflation. The annual payouts from the strategy are relatively fixed.

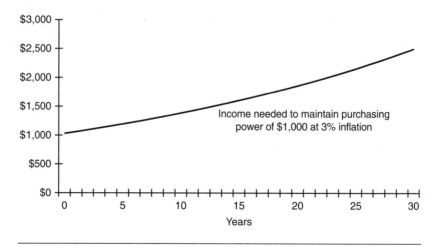

**FIGURE 2.1** How Inflation Erodes Fixed Income

Yet, inflation reduces the purchasing power of each dollar of income every year. When retirement lasts five years or less, the effect is small unless inflation is very high. When retirement lasts decades, the loss of purchasing power is significant even when inflation is historically low.

Many people are aware of the power of compound interest, which has been called the eighth wonder of the world. Over time, interest compounded amounts to a very large sum. Inflation works the same way in reverse. Its regular reduction of purchasing power compounds over time. A once-generous income can become inadequate to meet basic needs as shown in Figure 2.1.

Inflation smacks the income investor with a double whammy. Rising prices eat away at the purchasing power not only of the income but also of the principal. As the income is unable to maintain a standard of living over time, the owner might begin using principal to make up the difference. But over time the purchasing power of the principal is also declining. The principal cannot supplement the income to the extent envisioned when the strategy was first implemented. A further complication is that spending the principal reduces the future income since part of the principal no longer is invested and generating income.

An investment and spending strategy that does not adequately consider inflation can result in a portfolio death spiral.

To maintain purchasing power in the face of inflation, both the income and principal have to increase by at least the inflation rate each year. For example, if the desired income the first year is $40,000, after 15 years of two percent annual inflation over $53,000 of income is needed to maintain purchasing power.

The income-only-in-retirement portfolio strategy works if all the annual income is not spent. Instead, a portion of the income is reinvested in the portfolio so that it can generate higher future income. Suppose a portfolio generates $40,000 of income the first year and inflation is estimated to be 2 percent for the future. Suppose also that the portfolio is earning 6 percent interest. At 2 percent inflation $40,800 of income will be needed the following year. That means $13,333 must be added to the portfolio to generate an additional $800 of income.

To put it another way, the portfolio has to generate $53,333 of income the first year to provide the desired $40,000 of spendable income and the $13,333 that must be reinvested to maintain purchasing power. The investor cannot spend all the income generated by the portfolio if the goal is to maintain the purchasing power of the income over the long term and not spend principal.

## The Low-Yield World

The need to maintain purchasing power highlights a second disadvantage of this strategy. Interest rates began a steady, long-term decline in 1982. Rates have been at or near multidecade lows since the late 1990s. A portfolio that is invested to earn income will produce a fairly small amount of income, especially compared to what it would have earned in the early 1980s, as shown in Figure 2.2.

**FIGURE 2.2**   Ten-Year Treasury Bond Yield

Because of relatively low interest rates, most people cannot afford to invest solely for income. Market yields are not high enough to generate an income sufficient to meet their spending needs. A wealthy person with a relatively modest standard of living can live off the interest from a portfolio and still have enough to reinvest and maintain purchasing power. But for too many people yields simply are not high enough to generate enough cash flow to maintain the desired standard of living, even before considering the need to reinvest part of the income to preserve purchasing power.

The decline in interest rates since 1982 also reveals the third problem with this portfolio strategy.

Most income-oriented investments have a maturity date. Stocks do not mature. Once issued, they stay issued unless repurchased by the company and retired. That is not the case with most bonds and certificates of deposit. These investments have maturity dates. At maturity, the principal is returned to the investor. To continue receiving income, the investor must reinvest the principal.

When an income security matures after an interest rate decline, the investor is now hit with a triple whammy. Inflation already has reduced the purchasing power of both the principal and the interest. Now, the principal must be reinvested to earn a lower rate of interest, unless the investor is willing to take greater risk to earn a higher yield. So, in addition to suffering the reduction in purchasing power, the investor faces a reduction in the nominal dollars earned.

These effects were especially brutal to investors whose securities matured in 1998. This was the first time interest rates hit their post–World War II lows, and rates had dropped precipitously after 1994. Investors with bonds and CDs that had been paying 6 percent and more were faced with reinvesting to earn yields of 3 percent.

Interest rates cannot decline in the next 25 years as much as they declined from 1982 through 2006. However, in addition to a long-term interest rate trend, income investors could be harmed by a shorter-term cycle. Interest rates rise and fall with the economic cycle, Federal Reserve actions, and the outlook for inflation. When a security matures during the interest rate lows of this short-term cycle, the investor faces a loss in dollar income. The extent of this change in rates will be less than the long-term cyclical changes. But it will be real and will be in addition to the loss of purchasing power from inflation.

Interest rate fluctuations also can present a problem for the income investor who needs to sell bonds after interest rates have increased. When rates rise, the market values of bonds decline. The old bonds with lower interest rates are less valuable than new bonds with higher yields. The principal value will be returned in full when the bonds mature, but if the investment is sold before maturity, a loss would be incurred.

While once a venerable portfolio strategy, income investing in retirement should be used with caution. It can be appropriate when used for five years or less. For example, money that is being saved for a particular expense due within five years usually should be invested in securities that pay income and have a low probability that the value of the principal will fluctuate. For longer periods of time, the effects of inflation and changing interest rates mean it probably is better to use a balanced or growth portfolio.

Income investing for the long term is viable if the portfolio generates income that exceeds the investor's spending needs. The excess income can be reinvested to generate higher future income and maintain the investor's purchasing power.

For the rest of the investment world, this classic hedgehog strategy destroys wealth instead of building or preserving it.

## THE ALL-EQUITY PORTFOLIO

A number of hedgehogs shifted from the traditional income strategy to an even simpler strategy, one that gives the opposite advice to retirees. In fact, it gives both retirees and *pre*retirees the same advice. Supported by long-term data and the historic bull market of the 1980s and 1990s, these hedgehogs concluded that the best investment strategy is to invest 100 percent of a portfolio or close to that percentage in equities and other growth-oriented investments, regardless of one's age.

Younger investors frequently are told to invest primarily in equities. Stocks have the highest long-term returns of any investment asset. They are more volatile than other assets and experience periods of negative returns. But a young person has time on his or her side. The high long-term returns more than offset the volatility and negative periods, if the investor does not sell during the downturns.

The equities-only strategy advises an investor to retain the all-stock portfolio in both the preretirement and retirement years. The investor does not need income payments in order to have spending money. Total return should be the goal of the portfolio, and investors should shoot for the highest total return. If dividends and other income from the investments are not enough to pay for living expenses, shares of stocks or mutual funds are sold when cash is needed.

Stocks have a higher return than other investments over time and are good inflation hedges. Inflation, as we have seen, is the scourge of the income investor. The return of an all-stock portfolio over the long term will outpace inflation and maintain the owner's standard of living and purchasing power. Stock returns can be so much higher than bond returns that the all-stock portfolio should appreciate over time even after subtracting withdrawals to pay for the owner's living expenses. For example, $10,000 invested in the Standard & Poor's 500 stock index on January 31, 1973, would have increased to $291,238 by March 2001. The same amount invested in a portfolio of government bonds through the Lehman Brothers Long-Term Government Bond Index would have increased to only $124,976.

There are several ways to implement the all-stock portfolio.

The investor can buy a portfolio of equity mutual fund shares and hold them during the working years and into retirement. The funds' distributions of dividends, interest, and capital gains can be automatically reinvested during the working years. At retirement, the distributions can be paid in cash and spent. When spending needs exceed the distributions, enough fund shares are sold to cover the spending.

If individual shares of stock are held, the process is very similar. The difference is that with mutual funds fractions of shares can be sold. The retiree can receive the exact amount he or she needs and leave the rest invested. With individual shares, generally only whole shares of stock can be traded, and commissions might make it impractical to sell small amounts.

An alternative at retirement is to begin a check-a-month or an automatic distribution program. In these programs, the broker or mutual fund holding the shares will send the investor a regular check from his or her account for a predetermined amount. The check can be sent monthly or less frequently. The money backing the check comes first from recent distributions and from amounts in money market funds. If these are not enough to cover the check, investments automatically are sold until the account has cash equal to or exceeding the check's amount.

The automatic distribution program is more convenient for the investor. But the investor might lose control of tax consequences and the portfolio's allocation because of the automatic sales by the financial services company.

## An All-Equity Example—The Best Case

Perhaps the strongest case in favor of the all-equity portfolio used to be presented by the large mutual fund firm American Century using its *American Century Growth* fund, previously known as *Twentieth Century Growth* fund.

Suppose an investor retired and put $100,000 in the American Century Growth fund at the end of 1971, and a check-a-month program began the next year. The program paid $500 monthly the first year and increased the payout by 7.18 percent each year (roughly the rate of inflation at that time). All fund distributions were reinvested. By the end of 1998, the monthly payments would have climbed to $3,033. In addition, the value of the account would have grown to $4.4 million. By early 2000 the value of the account increased to just under $6 million. This presents a concrete example of how the all-equity strategy delivers to a retiree both higher income and a greater net worth over time.

This is perhaps the strongest case for the all-stock portfolio. The Twentieth Century Growth fund was one of the great funds of the 1970s and 1980s, when it scored phenomenal returns. Its returns consistently exceeded the market indexes and those of most other mutual funds during that period and into the bull market of the 1980s.

In addition, that period was a great time to be invested in stocks, since it included the strongest bull market in modern history.

Yet, when examined in detail, the example also reveals the drawbacks of the strategy.

It is easy to use historic data to compute that stocks have an average annual return of about 10 percent annually. Plugging that number into a model would reveal the level of annual spending one could safely incur in retirement without running out of money.

That long-term average annual return, however, is not derived from a series of steady annual returns. Instead, it is the result of highly variable returns. In fact, more years than not the market either rises or falls by more than 20 percent from the prior year's closing level. Several consecutive years of annual returns exceeding 20 percent can build both the portfolio and confidence in the strategy. But beginning retirement with one or more years of 20 percent declines could cause anxiety and worse. It is easy to look back after a decade or more and see how the program worked out. It is more difficult to be saddled with a significant portfolio loss only a year or two into retirement and be reading only bad news about the markets and the economy.

## The Need for Fortitude

The example begins in the midst of one of the worst long-term, or secular, bear markets in modern market history. From 1966 to 1982, the major market indexes essentially ended the period at the same levels they reached at the start of the period. The Dow Jones Industrial Average first closed above 1,000 in 1966. It quickly retreated and did not close above 1,000 to stay until 1982. During the period there were numerous sharp declines and rises in the market indexes.

These minibull and -bear markets usually last from 6 months to 24 months.

The very nasty bear market of 1972 to 1974 began shortly after the investment in this example. The major market indexes declined about 50 percent during that bear market. The value of the investor's account would have declined from $100,000 at the end of 1971 to $64,065 at the end of 1974, after both withdrawals and the market decline. The portfolio would not reach the $100,000 level again until well into 1976.

It would take great fortitude to continue with this program after the portfolio lost more than 40 percent of its value in the first two years and lost over half its initial value at the market's low point. Most people would change strategies, probably near the market bottom. Imagine having just retired, given up the ability to generate wage income for the rest of one's life, and needing the nest egg to last the rest of one's years. Then, half of that nest egg evaporates in the next two years. Most people enter retirement with the idea that they do not want to be spending their principal for at least a few years. A market decline in the first years of retirement means the retiree must begin spending principal early.

It is easy to look back now and see that the investment more than recovered, and that loss was a small blip in the long-term growth of the portfolio. But in 1974, President Nixon had resigned, inflation raged, the economy was doing poorly, and unemployment ran high. Stocks were at about half of their historic high, which was reached in 1966. It was difficult to find positive news about stocks or the economy. That is true of almost all market declines. Bad news predominates. A person must be able to ignore current events, focus on the long term, and have confidence that the markets will recover in time to restore the portfolio and meet one's goals.

In these circumstances, many people would abandon the strategy. They would have sold the stocks and invested the proceeds in safer investments. Doing so, of course, would eliminate any possibility of recovering the losses or of making the portfolio last for the rest of retirement at the same spending level. It would be the only way to end the anxiety over the possibility of additional losses. If the first few years of retirement are accompanied by strong market returns, subsequent portfolio losses can be endured more easily because a cushion would have been built. When the start of retirement coincides with the early stages of a bear market, many investors would lose confidence in the strategy. The markets do not even have to experience a bear market or a long period of decline to shake confidence. Even a correction of 10 percent to 15 percent in the first year or two of retirement will send many investors searching for alternative strategies.

Here are some examples of how severe stock losses can be. The NASDAQ's worst annual loss was just under 40 percent in 2000. The cumulative loss for the S&P 500 from March 31, 2000 through March 31, 2003 was 40.9 percent. From its peak to trough, the S&P 500 had declined 51 percent. The numbers for the NASDAQ were worse: 70.5 percent and 77.9 percent. International market indexes had returns similar to those of the S&P 500. The NASDAQ's next two worst calendar years were a 30 percent drop in 1973 followed by a loss of over 30 percent the following year. The Dow Jones Industrial Average's worst year was a 27.6 percent loss in 1974, preceded by its third worst year with a loss of about 15 percent in 1973.

Indeed, even after the American Century Growth fund generated high returns for a long time and built a sizeable cushion, it suffered high losses after the technology stock bubble burst in 2000. The value of the hypothetical portfolio in the example slipped from about $6 million to $5 million in only one year from 2000 to 2001. The fund lost 14.71 percent in 2000, 18.67 percent in 2001, and 26.13 percent in 2002. At its low point in 2002 the fund had lost more than half of its peak value in 2000. That still provides an impressive return for the investor who purchased the fund in 1971. It is, however, a substantial diminution in wealth from the peak, and the fund's performance would be devastating to someone who purchased it in the late 1990s.

Not many investors can stick with the all-equity program in the face of such serious market losses. Both the emotional and financial costs are too much to endure.

There are time periods during which an all-equity portfolio would result in high returns, a comfortable retirement, and a significant legacy for heirs. Still, there is no way of knowing in advance if an investor will live in such a time period. The consequences of using the strategy in the wrong time period can result in a serious decline in one's standard of living.

## Can It Be Duplicated?

Even if an investor has the fortitude to ride out a market downturn, as in the American Century Growth example, the results of using this strategy will not be as positive for all investors as the example indicates.

American Century Growth is a unique fund. During the 1970s and 1980s, it performed as one of the stellar mutual funds, earning returns far exceeding those of the market indexes and most other mutual funds. This fund also is the longest lasting of the top-performing growth funds. Other funds had better returns in different time periods. But they were not able to survive market downturns or earn high returns again in the ensuing recoveries. They folded or were merged into other funds.

To get the same results as in the example, an investor needed the wisdom or good fortune to select such a superior fund (or individual stocks with similar returns). An investor in a poorly performing fund, or even one of the many mediocre funds, would not have done as well. Indeed, Twentieth Century Growth's relative performance deteriorated in the 1990s. It outperformed the S&P 500 only two years between 1996 and 2006. An investor who began investing in the fund after the 1980s would not be nearly as satisfied as one who purchased the fund in 1971.

It is easy in hindsight to pick an ideal fund for following the strategy. It is more difficult to pick such a fund at the start of the strategy. To emulate the results in this example, an investor would need to locate a fairly small growth fund that earns outsized returns early in its life and survives with above average returns for many years. Unfortunately, when surveying the available funds the investor could easily select a fund that generates a few years of great returns, and then disappears in the first bear market. Perhaps the manager leaves the fund and the successor is not as skilled. Or perhaps the manager was lucky in the early years, and the luck runs out. Those were the results at many growth mutual funds over the years. In Twentieth Century Growth fund's early years there were a number of other aggressive growth stock funds that had very high returns. Few of them survived the market declines and recovered to the extent that the Twentieth Century fund did.

A more realistic example has been presented by the mutual fund firm T. Rowe Price. Instead of using its top-performing fund, Price selected a diversified portfolio that had a high average annualized return over the long term. The investor initiated that portfolio and began taking withdrawals in 1968. He had to endure several more years of the bear market than the American Century Investor did. Because principal withdrawals began a few years earlier and because the portfolio did not have the exceptional returns in the market recovery of the Twentieth Century Growth fund, the hypothetical investor ran out of money by 1982.

The all-stock portfolio can work for retirees and preretirees. To make it work, the investor needs a fortuitous combination of timing, exceptional investment selection, and the fortitude and resources to maintain the program in terrible markets. Even if the investor does everything right, the strategy could be doomed by the misfortune of retiring in the early stages of a long-term bear market.

The biggest obstacles to this program are the wrong investments, the investor's emotions, and the markets. While it works great on paper, there is a great deal of uncertainty involved. Most uncertain of all are the investor's emotions. How many retirees and pre-retirees can sleep well and maintain a 100 percent equity portfolio while the stock market is steadily losing value?

## THE 60/40 SPLIT

For many years, the standard institutional portfolio and one often recommended to individual investors was a hybrid of the invest-for-income and the all-equity portfolio strategies. The recommendation was to invest 60 percent of a portfolio in U.S. stocks and 40 percent in U.S. bonds. Conservative investors, or those in retirement, were advised to reverse the allocations. Many institutional investors, such as pension funds, were advised to follow this strategy. For a while, the 60/40 mix or its counterpart 40/60 mix was considered to be a requirement to meet the fiduciary duties of trustees overseeing pension funds and trust accounts.

The idea behind this mix is that stocks provide the long-term growth needed to maintain purchasing power in the face of inflation. Bonds provide income and stability. In addition, the combination of stocks and bonds provides diversification. When stocks are declining, the bonds should at least maintain their value. The combination of the two assets would avoid the wide swings of an all-stock portfolio and provide higher long-term returns than an income portfolio.

This hedgehog strategy, too, fell by the wayside. Over time, the fixed 60/40 allocation strategy failed to perform as expected.

In the 1960s and the 1970s, stocks declined sharply. Yet bonds did not provide the expected counterbalance. As inflation and interest rates rose, bond prices fell as a result along with stock prices. Instead of remaining stable while stocks declined, bonds also lost value. Bonds, in fact, became known in some circles of *certificates of confiscation.* The hedgehog theory that stocks and bonds moved in opposite directions proved to be false.

When stocks began another long bull market in 1982, the 60/40 portfolio again generated unsatisfactory results. Bonds also began a long-term bull market after 1981, but the bond returns were less than those of stocks. In addition, bonds and stocks often experienced price declines at the same time during the period, again disproving the theory that stocks and bonds counterbalance each other.

The 60/40 portfolio did not provide the long-term goals of institutional investors to protect capital in bear markets, maintain purchasing power in the face of inflation, and meet the spending goals of their portfolios.

There are a number of balanced mutual funds that maintain primarily the 60 percent stocks and 40 percent bonds mix. Some of these are excellent investments for the right investors, such as Dodge & Cox Balanced and Vanguard Wellington. But the 60/40 mix is not the panacea investors were led to expect. Even investors who are satisfied with these mutual funds usually own other investments as well.

## NO TIME FOR HEDGEHOGS

Time and experience demonstrated the shortcomings of these established hedgehog portfolio strategies. None of them produces satisfactory results all the time. Indeed, each of these strategies has times when following it substantially reduces the investor's wealth and puts his or her financial independence in jeopardy. The problem for many investors is that they adopt the strategy that worked best in the recent past. That is usually the worst time to adopt an investment strategy.

Because of the shortfalls of the strategies described, hedgehogs sought another strategy. Finance academics were busy documenting the shortcomings of prevailing investment strategies and working to establish alternatives. These academics were the source of a new hedgehog strategy that became dominant in the investment world.

# CHAPTER 3

# THE MODERN HEDGEHOG THEORY

Investment strategies were much simpler before academics, mathematicians, and computers became major influences on the process. In the previous chapters, we examined a few simple strategies. The failure of those strategies to deliver acceptable performance led to new ideas by many of those aforementioned academics. What they came up with is definitely more sophisticated and elegant than other hedgehog investment strategies. Their *modern hedgehog strategy*, as I call it, cannot be implemented without computers and complex software and is backed by a high level of thinking. Nevertheless, all that sophistication did not produce the results all investors were expecting and had unintended consequences.

Traditionally, investments drew little academic attention until relatively recently. Economists tended to focus on issues affecting the economy in general or the actions of firms and individuals. Finance professors directed their attention at corporate finance. The study of choices affecting investors in the financial markets was left to firms investing their own funds or advising investors.

Then, in the 1950s, investments began to attract the professors.

Most of the early academic work on investments was interesting, but it was not considered practical. The work was presented in formats that were not accessible to individual investors or even most professional investors. Because the research was heavy in higher-level mathematics and required a large number of calculations, even sophisticated individuals and institutions concluded that it was impossible or impractical to act on the theories. Thus, even if the proposals were theoretically correct, they could not be implemented. In addition, the original research was often developed by academics not involved with or even interested in the investment markets. Some made abstract observations about market behavior that researchers only developed later into concepts that could be applied by investors.

Other researchers focused their energy on other topics and wrote about investment issues—but only as a sideline. In effect, little was done to fully develop or promote practical investment insights.

## WALL STREET NOTICES THE ACADEMY

Two factors essentially changed attitudes in the investment community toward the academic research: The unexpected behavior of national economies and simultaneous changes in investment markets. As discussed in Chapter 2, established investment strategies failed to perform as expected or to adapt to economic changes. The economic and investment environment of the 1960s and 1970s was vastly different from anything in prior experience or that was anticipated. The period had a devastating effect on investment portfolios. For that reason, those managing investments sought new ideas for protecting their capital.

Regulatory changes also ushered in a new era of financial innovation. Previous regulations were developed in the aftermath of the Great Depression and were intended to protect investors. One way they did that was to limit investment choices and the products that could be offered in the markets. The 1970s demonstrated that the available investments were not sufficient to meet the needs of investors. As these regulations were changed, financial services firms discovered that ideas for new products and strategies lay unused in various academic journals. Many of these ideas eventually found their way into the markets. The regulatory changes also increased the number of people investing in the markets and the amount of money invested. This flow of new investors and capital created a demand for good investment advice.

Another source of change was the flood of money into pension funds and, through them, into the markets. Pensions originally were promises made to reward long-term employees. Not funded in advance, employers could change such promises at any time, and employees who left before retirement age received nothing. The Employee Retirement Income Security Act of 1974 increased the amount of advance funding required by corporate pension plans and provided some protections for employees. The funding requirements dramatically increased the amount of capital held by both corporate and government pension plans. As the population and economy boomed and the work force aged, pension funds grew. Prior to 1974, the profession of pension fund consulting hardly existed. Now, it helps manage trillions of dollars. Those responsible for managing all the pension fund money needed better ideas and strategies.

Technology was foremost among the reasons why academic ideas drew more attention and resulted in even more academic research. Initially, the calculations required to implement these ideas could not be done manually. Even on the computers that were available in the 1960s and 1970s, the calculations required a great deal of time. Only large mainframe computers could make the calculations. Time on those computers had to be leased from large firms, and that time was expensive. Gradually, prices for computers and software declined. In addition, the speed and capacity of computers increased. Now, almost anyone is able to perform in a few minutes, on a desktop or laptop computer, the sophisticated calculations that a few decades ago were impractical for all but the largest corporate pension plans.

A related change was the development and availability of databases of historic investment returns. The calculations in the new investment models are made using databases of past returns for different investment assets. This data was not kept in good order over the years and often had to be researched and re-created, which was done only after the usefulness of the data became clear. Now, databases of these returns can be purchased and manipulated on a personal computer at a relatively low cost. The combined affordability of the databases, personal computers, and software made it possible to implement the academic theories.

This confluence of events, coupled with the foundation of a rational theory upon which to build, resulted in the modern hedgehog investment strategy known generally as Modern Portfolio Theory (MPT), the Capital Asset Pricing Model (CAPM), or mean-variance analysis. Widespread use of the strategy was assured when two of its developers shared the Nobel Prize in economics in 1990.

Many investors today use some variation of the strategy, often without realizing it. Software programs that give investment recommendations, including those offered on web sites, most likely are using CAPM. Recommendations by financial planners, brokers, and mutual fund firms also often are made using CAPM software and models. Many institutional investors, such as pension funds, also have used CAPM to develop their investment strategies.

Though MPT, CAPM and mean-variance analysis often are considered interchangeable terms for the same concept, there actually are two different concepts. MPT came first, developed by one of those Nobel winners, Harry Markowitz. CAPM, also known as *mean-variance analysis*, was developed by the other, William Sharpe, during his postgraduate work, with Markowitz serving as Sharpe's advisor. Markowitz has expressed disagreement with some of the fundamentals of CAPM and apparently does not care for the two terms to be considered synonyms. He believes MPT is a standalone theory. MPT is more of a fox strategy as we shall see in this and following chapters, while CAPM is for hedgehogs.

## MODERN PORTFOLIO THEORY

Before Markowitz and MPT, investment strategies tended to focus primarily on returns and also on individual securities. The academic research and publications on the subject were relatively sparse. MPT introduced several additional concepts that seem obvious today but were novel at the time.

MPT asserts that risk is at least as important to the investor as returns or potential returns. The typical academic investment research at the time focused on the process of analyzing securities to identify those with the highest potential return. Logically, if an investor had confidence in the process, he would purchase only the one security that was determined to have the highest potential return. Investors did not and do not purchase only one security, however, because they know that no investment selection process is infallible. There is the risk of loss any time a security is purchased, and people are averse to risk and to losses. Therefore, investors should be interested in risk and strategies for reducing risk.

As the name implies, MPT advises the investor to focus on the selection of an entire portfolio rather than individual securities. In particular, Markowitz explored how to balance risk and potential return to select a portfolio that is likely to achieve the investor's return goals without taking more risk than the investor desires.

Under MPT, risk is reduced through diversification. Instead of purchasing one security, an investor purchases multiple securities. But simply buying a number of securities is not sufficient to reduce risk. Instead, the investor must focus on how the securities perform relative to each other. In particular, the portfolio should be composed of securities that have a low "covariance" or correlation with each other. This also is referred to as the correlation coefficient.

For example, an investor purchases a portfolio of two dozen stocks. But all of the stocks are in the same industry or related industries. This provides some risk reduction, because it is likely that firms in the industry will not have identical economic results. The quality of management and differences in products or services will cause differences in revenues and earnings, but most of the results at each company are likely to be affected by general industry trends more than any other factor. When the industry enters a downturn, all the companies in the portfolio will decline even if they do not decline to the same extent.

To achieve risk-reducing diversification, a portfolio of stocks should consist of companies from different industries that have unsynchronized good and bad times. An extreme example would be a two-stock portfolio of a technology company and a mining company. These industries tend to have bull markets and bear markets at different times and are influenced by different economic factors.

This process can produce counterintuitive or unexpected results. For example, an investor can select a group of stocks, each of which has a high degree of risk by itself. If the stocks have a low correlation to each other, a portfolio of these stocks has lower risk than any of the individual stocks and probably a lower risk than a stock market index. Because the securities are in bull markets and bear markets at different times, a group of high risk assets that are uncorrelated with each other can be combined into a low risk portfolio that generates fairly steady returns.

That leaves the investor with two problems to solve.

The first problem is security selection. How does the investor determine which securities are likely to have high potential returns? Markowitz suggested using the dividend discount model. This involves forecasting future dividends paid to owners of a security and using a discount rate (or interest rate) to compute a present value for those payments. The securities with the highest values under this model would be eligible for the portfolio.

The second problem is using the list of securities with high potential returns to build a portfolio. To solve this problem, Markowitz introduced the concept of the *efficient portfolio*, which still is in use today. The efficient portfolio is the portfolio that gives the investor the best trade-off between risk and return compared to the possible

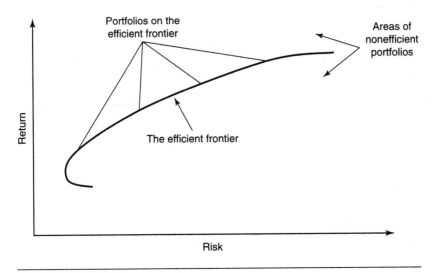

**Figure 3.1**   The Efficient Frontier and Portfolio

alternative portfolios the investor could select. The investor wants the portfolio with the highest potential return for a given level of risk, or the lowest risk for a desired rate of return as shown in Figure 3.1.

To find the efficient portfolio, the investor first has to compute the expected risk and return for each possible portfolio that could be built using the securities under consideration. These calculations are used to derive a graph with the *efficient frontier*. For each level of return, there is one efficient portfolio that has the lowest level of risk for that rate of return. Those portfolios together form the efficient frontier. Each point on the efficient frontier line is the efficient portfolio for that rate of return and level of risk. Then the investor selects the portfolio with the most desirable combination of risk and return for him—the efficient portfolio.

Markowitz suggested using linear programming to perform the calculations. The number of calculations required to implement MPT is enormous, and doing that many calculations was not easy at the time. Before performing the calculations, an investor needed to identify the potential return from an asset and its risk level. Then, the covariance or correlation of each asset to each of the other potential investments had to be determined. After these numbers were derived for each investment under consideration, the MPT calculations were made. Performing this task in the 1950s and 1960s required the use of a mainframe computer. This was very expensive and, by today's standards, a very slow process.

Because of the practical problems, investors were slow to pay attention to MPT. Academics rarely cited Markowitz as a source for many years, and professional investors also largely ignored the work. Markowitz, however, developed several principles that were adopted and are used effectively by investors regardless of their strategies:

- Risk should be as much a focus as return in investment decisions.
- Risk can be reduced by diversification.
- Diversification best reduces risk when the assets in a portfolio have return patterns that are not correlated with each other.
- The risk and return profile of the total portfolio should be more important to an investor than the profiles of individual assets in the portfolio.

## THE CAPITAL ASSET PRICING MODEL

Changes in technology and the markets were not the only factors that brought more attention to MPT. In 1960 a student named William Sharpe began work under Markowitz's direction to simplify the MPT calculations. This research led to a number of developments in addition to simplified calculations, culminating in what is known as the Capital Asset Pricing Model or mean-variance analysis and is widely used today.

Sharpe's first step was to sidestep the need to make calculations for each potential security to be considered for a portfolio. Instead, for each security there is a factor that is very influential in the security's performance. For stocks and bonds, the primary factor determining price changes is the appropriate market index. The primary factor for large company stocks, for example, usually is the Standard & Poor's 500 Index, though there are alternatives, such as the Russell 1000 Index. A small company stock index, such as the Russell 2000 or S&P 600, is the primary factor determining the performance of the stocks of smaller companies. The Lehman Brothers Aggregate Bond Index is the primary influence on bond prices.

Substituting an index for individual securities means that far fewer calculations are required to determine the efficient portfolio. Instead of performing calculations for dozens or hundreds of securities, the investor needs to make calculations only for the indexes of the asset classes that are being considered for the portfolio. The results might not be as precise as making the calculations for each security, but the results would be close enough that the greater efficiency of using indexes instead of individual securities justifies the substitution.

Indexes can be used instead of securities because the markets are fairly efficient, Sharpe argued. The direct relationship between an individual stock and an index varies. The performance of some stocks is closely tied to the index, but in general about one third of the performance of an individual stock is determined by the movements of the index. The rest of the performance is attributed to the movements of stocks in that company's industry and to characteristics of the individual company and its stock. But as more stocks are added to a portfolio, the differences of the individual stocks are diluted. The movement of all the stocks in the portfolio as a whole will closely match the performance of the index, especially if the investor attempts to construct a diversified portfolio.

Portfolio construction under CAPM focuses on asset classes: U.S. large company stocks, U.S. small company stocks, developed market international stocks, emerging market international stocks, and the like. Determining an efficient portfolio requires calculations for only a relatively small number of indexes instead of for all the securities in those indexes.

The development of personal computers made implementing CAPM even easier, because speed and sizeable memory were needed to perform even the simplified calculations under CAPM. PCs became affordable, widely available, and more robust. Software was developed so that anyone who could operate a PC could perform the calculations. The software is known generically as the *portfolio optimizer.* Today many individuals and institutions use optimizers to implement CAPM and guide their investment decisions. The software produces "the efficient frontier," showing the portfolio that returns the highest return for a given level of risk or the lowest risk for a desired level of return. The investor can select the portfolio with the risk and return profile that comes closest to meeting the investor's goals, which is the efficient portfolio for that investor.

## The CAPM Revolution

The simplification of the calculations and increase in computer power were but two factors in making CAPM more widely accepted than MPT was. At least equally important as we discussed were the turbulence in the economy and markets in the 1960s and 1970s. Traditional investment strategies were not producing the results that were expected, and investment professionals searched for alternative ways to build portfolios. Further, the additional attention from investment professionals and increased computer power spurred more academic research. In a short time, a rather rich body of research developed from the foundations of MPT and CAPM.

CAPM today is much more than substituting indexes for individual securities while searching for an efficient portfolio. The notions of index efficiency and market efficiency led to several other principles that are part of CAPM.

First, investors and money managers cannot reliably or consistently earn higher returns than a market index. This is known as the Efficient Market Hypothesis (EMH).

Research consistently shows that a minority of mutual funds and money managers outperform the index in any year, and very few consistently earn higher returns than the index or for periods longer than one year.

There are several possible reasons for this result. Active money management that seeks to earn a higher return than an index incurs costs. There are brokerage commissions from buying and selling securities. The money manager charges a fee. In taxable accounts, taxes must be paid on dividends and when a security is sold at a gain, something that occurs more frequently in managed portfolios than in index funds. In addition, the free flow of information and general efficiency of the markets makes it difficult for an investor to achieve an information edge to identify a portfolio of stocks that will outperform the index.

The recommendation in CAPM is that an investor should invest in an asset class only through an index fund. While this was difficult in the early years of CAPM's development, it is easy today. Numerous index funds exist in both traditional open-end mutual funds and in the recently developed exchange-traded funds. An investor can purchase broad-based U.S. stock index funds as well as funds tracking various sectors and subsets of the U.S. stock market. An investor also can invest in international stocks by purchasing a fund that tracks a broad international stock index or through different funds that track the indexes of separate countries or regions. Index funds also have been developed for other assets such as bonds and commodities.

Under CAPM, an investor should decide which investment asset classes should be in the portfolio and purchase index funds to invest in those asset classes. Individual security selection is not considered a fruitful activity. Next, once established, the efficient portfolio should not be changed unless the risk or return targets change. In other words, the efficient portfolio is a buy-and-hold portfolio. The exception to this is periodic rebalancing of the portfolio. After the portfolio is created, market activity will change the allocation. For example, a portfolio might be 60 percent invested in stocks and 40 percent in bonds. After one year, stocks might increase 10 percent while bonds decline 3 percent. That would change the allocation to 63 percent stocks and 37 percent bonds. This might seem like a small difference from the original allocation, but it is not the efficient portfolio so it will not produce the expected results. In addition, if the portfolio is not rebalanced to its original allocation, the portfolio will drift further from the efficient portfolio each year. To avoid this and achieve the expected results, periodically the investor should buy and sell assets to return the portfolio to its target allocation.

Other than rebalancing, changes in the portfolio are not advisable. Just as an efficient stock market makes it difficult for an investor to select securities that will earn higher returns than the index, it also makes it difficult for an investor to rotate a portfolio among different asset classes at opportune times to earn higher returns. Altering the asset allocation of the portfolio often is called market timing by advocates of CAPM. Advocates of the process refer to it as *tactical asset allocation.*

A properly constructed efficient portfolio produces the best risk-and-return combination. If investors are unable to identify those factors that make an individual stock or a collection of individual stocks generate higher returns than the market index, they also are unlikely to be able to identify factors that will earn returns exceeding those of the efficient portfolio by periodically increasing and decreasing the allocations of the different asset classes in the portfolio.

Asset performance is divided between beta and alpha. Beta is the performance of an asset relative to an index. For example, a stock with a beta of 1.0 to the S&P 500 rises and falls exactly as much as that index. A stock with a beta of 0.50 fluctuates half as much as the index. If the index rises 10 percent, the stock is likely to rise 5 percent. If the index declines 10 percent, the stock will decline only 5 percent. Another expression for beta is the volatility of the portfolio relative to a benchmark.

Alpha is a measure of an investment manager's skill or, when applying it to a stock, it is a measure of how much better it performs than the benchmark. To determine alpha, start with excess return. That is the difference between the investment's return and a benchmark's return. In some discussions of investment results, alpha is considered synonymous with excess return. In the development of CAPM, however, alpha is the risk-adjusted excess return. If a mutual fund manager earns a higher return than the index by taking more risk, alpha could be negative. But if the manager earns a higher return after making a mathematical adjustment for the risk taken, alpha is positive and the manager is considered to have used skill to beat the benchmark.

Alpha is the return earned independent of an index's return and by taking the same level of risk. Determining alpha is especially useful when evaluating an investment manager or mutual fund. Alpha is a measure of the skill a manager demonstrates to add returns beyond the index's returns. A mutual fund with an alpha of 0.2 has earned a return 20 percent greater than an index return. If the index returns 10 percent, the manager earns 12 percent.

Investors should be careful not to confuse alpha and beta. A stock or a mutual fund might have a high beta, say 1.5. That means when the index is up 10 percent, the stock or fund is up 15 percent.

Investors during a bull market often confuse such beta with alpha. The problem is that during market downturns, a high-beta asset will lose more than the index. If the index is down 10 percent, the stock or fund will lose 15 percent. Only then will the investor realize he or she purchased beta instead of alpha.

Most investors take this information to mean that they should seek stocks or managers with high alphas. CAPM, however, asserts that the markets are efficient. Stocks with high alphas are more desirable and therefore will trade at higher prices. Stocks with low alphas will trade at lower prices. The price differences will offset the differences in alphas, so there is no advantage over time in owning a high-alpha stock. In addition, money managers with positive alphas are rare, difficult to identify in advance, and aren't likely to repeat their positive alpha performance over time. The advice from CAPM is to own the entire market instead of searching for attractively valued parts of the market or for managers who try to beat the benchmark.

## CRITICISMS OF CAPM

CAPM gradually captured much of the investment world during the 1980s and 1990s. The factors discussed earlier were important in spreading the adoption of CAPM. Another important factor was the bull market in stocks that ran from 1982 to 2000. CAPM is ideal for a bull market. Buying and holding a portfolio of market indexes can maximize returns during an extended bull market.

Yet the bear market that began in 2000 exposed shortcomings in CAPM that had received some attention from researchers but were largely overlooked or minimized by most investors during the bull market. Most of the disadvantages of CAPM occur because investors must operate in periods that are shorter than the long term.

The research supporting CAPM used data covering very long periods. During shorter periods, the superiority of CAPM over other strategies is not as clear, and there are other strategies that clearly are superior to CAPM during periods shorter than the very long run.

## Buy-and-Hold Fixation

Efficient market theory holds that no one can have useful information that is unavailable to other investors. Other ways of expressing the theory are that all useful information is quickly reflected in market prices, or that the actual price of a security at any point in time is a good estimate of its intrinsic value. It makes little sense to change a portfolio's allocation based on perceived or expected changes in a market or markets. As CAPM was explained and practiced by most advocates during the bull market, once the efficient portfolio was determined, that portfolio should be held indefinitely.

The efficient portfolio is the one that provides the best risk-return trade-off over the long term. Most portfolio optimizers use data covering 70 years or so for U.S. stock markets and shorter periods for many other assets.

Unfortunately, the portfolio that is best over the long term will not necessarily be the best during shorter periods, even if the shorter periods are fairly long periods of 10 or 20 years. While an asset has a particular long-term return and risk level, those qualities are not constant from year to year or in many cases over periods other than the very long term. Instead, there are fluctuations in the values. The returns and risk over any period tend to differ significantly from the long-term averages. Stocks, in particular, have a history of extended bull markets and bear markets that combine to determine the long-term averages.

The long-term data show that stocks, especially U.S. stocks, are the highest-returning investment. The return of stocks over bonds is high, producing what is known as an *equity risk premium* (ERP). The amount of the ERP varies depending on who is doing the estimate and the time period used, but it is generally stated as being between 4 percent and 6 percent. But further analysis shows that most of that excess return was compacted into limited periods. Take out the 32 years from 1950 to 1981, and the superiority of stocks declines to about three percentage points. During the 1950–1981 period, inflation was rising. Rising inflation causes interest rates to rise and bond prices to fall. It could be that most of the long-term equity risk premium is due primarily to the hard times bonds experienced due to rising inflation in that period.

Many investors remember the stock bull market from 1982 through 2000. What they often overlook is that bonds also did quite well during that period as inflation and interest rates declined. In fact, bonds had higher returns than stocks in about 40 percent of the calendar years during that period.

Discrete economic and financial events in each period cause investment returns to differ greatly from the long-term averages. Since investors live in those discrete periods and not in the long term, relying on long-term data can be hazardous unless the investor happens to live in a time when the returns are equal to or better than the long-term averages. Investors would do well to keep in mind that until 1950 bonds had lower yields than stocks and were considered much less risky. Stocks had to offer dividend yields exceeding bond interest rates in order to attract investors.

If the markets truly were efficient, there would not be long-term, or secular, bull markets or bear markets. There also would not be rapid price changes within short periods of time. In addition, stocks would rise and fall closely in line with changes in fundamental factors such as earnings, economic growth, and interest rates, and valuations would be constant. Reality, however, does not match the theory and the differences can cause an investor's results to be vastly different from what was indicated by the efficient portfolio calculations.

When a portfolio optimizer uses long-term data to derive an efficient portfolio, fairly risky assets with high long-term returns such as stocks usually are a large percentage of the portfolio unless the investor asks for a portfolio with very low risk. The reasons for this result are that over the long term the returns from these risky assets are high enough to justify their risks and the only way to achieve a given level of return is to assume a certain level of risk.

The problem is that few investors invest for the long term of 70 years or so. For most investors, the long term is 10 years to 20 years. If their portfolios earn much less than expected during that period, they will not meet their lifetime investment goals.

This shortcoming of the buy-and-hold aspect of CAPM became apparent to both individual and institutional investors after 2000. Most stock indexes peaked in early 2000 and incurred significant losses by late 2002. The NASDAQ lost over 70 percent from its peak value. Other indexes had lower but still significant losses. More important than the extent of the losses is the amount of time needed to recover from such losses. As of February 2007, the Dow Jones Industrial Average ("the Dow") was the only major U.S. stock index that had returned to and exceeded the peak levels of 2000. The Dow does not include dividends paid, so investors actually had a positive return after something less than the six years indicated by a straightforward tracking of the index's value. But after adjusting for inflation, the purchasing power losses were more extended. Investors in the S&P 500 and NASDAQ Indexes fared worse. The NASDAQ was still about 50 percent below its peak, and the S&P 500 was still below its record high almost seven years earlier, even after reinvested dividends.

Pension funds saw their funding levels decline significantly. Required contribution rates had dramatic increases, forcing employers to increase the amount of money they contributed at the same time that a recession was decreasing their revenues. For individuals, progress toward achieving goals such as funding retirement was stymied.

The consequences of holding a fixed portfolio, known as a policy portfolio, were so severe that former advocates of CAPM began to retreat. Markowitz made clear that his MPT was different than CAPM and that he did not advocate a fixed portfolio allocation. The efficient portfolio under MPT depended on the investor's forecast of the risk and return for the different potential assets, not on historic returns. Markowitz pointed out that in his early work he stated that it was the investor's responsibility to forecast future returns, and a portfolio should be changed when expected future returns change. Peter L. Bernstein, a strong advocate of CAPM and the policy portfolio, gave a speech in 2003 that attracted wide attention among institutional investors because he seemed to declare the fixed policy portfolio dead.

## The Moving Target

Data are critical to implementing CAPM. The investor needs to know the risk and return of the different assets considered for the portfolio. In addition, the correlation or covariance of each asset to each of the others must be determined. If individual managers instead of index funds are used, the beta and alpha of each manager should be used in the calculations. As we have discussed, most investors and advisors who develop portfolios under CAPM simply use historic results for these numbers. Some use history as a guide but use their judgment to modify some of the numbers.

A problem many investors encounter in practice is that these numbers change over time. The correlations of assets to each other change. Both absolute and relative returns of the asset classes change, as does the risk of each asset. A consequence is that the efficient portfolio for a given risk and return combination changes based on when the calculations are made. A recommended efficient portfolio from early 1982 would have been heavily weighted toward real estate and precious metals. The calculation would have used historic data and reached this recommendation because those assets were nearing the end of extended bull markets while stocks and bonds had been in bear markets. Figure 3.2 shows different efficient portfolios using data from different time periods. It was developed for mutual fund firm Rydex Investments by Dr. John Mulvey of Princeton University and shows that the efficient portfolio changes because risk premiums and economic conditions change.

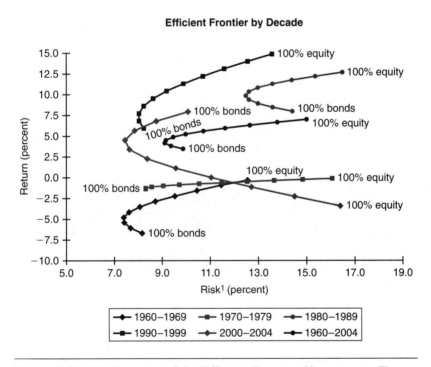

**FIGURE 3.2** The Location of the Efficient Frontier Changes over Time

*Source:* John Mulvey, "Essential Portfolio Theory," white paper, Princeton University. Copyright © 2006 Rydex Investments, www.rydexinvestments.com.

In the late 1990s, it was difficult to make a portfolio optimizer produce a portfolio that had significant allocations to assets other than stocks because of the post-1982 bull market. The more volatile the equity investments were, the more the optimizer liked them. Emerging market stocks and private equity would be most of a portfolio if the optimizer were not given limits.

The correlations of assets to each other also change over time. A simple but instructive example is to compare the correlation of U.S. equities with bonds. Traditional thinking is that adding bonds to a portfolio of stocks provides diversification, because bonds are not highly correlated with stocks. But a careful study shows that the correlation level changes over time. At times they do move in different directions. At other times, they move in tandem. Figure 3.3, also prepared by Dr. Mulvey for Rydex Investments, shows how the correlation of these two assets changes over time. Note that this figure shows the dramatic drop prior to and during the recession of the early 2000s.

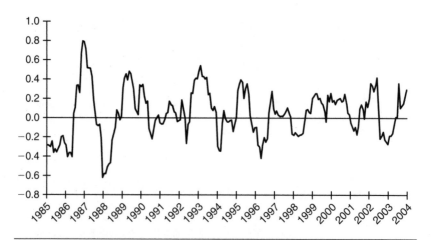

**Figure 3.3** Rolling Correlation of Weekly Returns Between S&P 500 Index and 10-Year U.S. Government Bond Index

Source: John Mulvey, "Essential Portfolio Theory," white paper, Princeton University. Copyright © 2006 Rydex Investments, www.rydexinvestments.com.

One theory is that the correlation of the two assets varies with investors' primary concern of the moment. When inflation is the primary worry of investors, there is a higher correlation between stocks and bonds. Both assets are likely to decline when investors believe inflation is heading higher. Bonds will decline more because the higher interest rates that are caused by inflation hurt them more than stocks. Both assets, however, usually decline when inflation seems to be rising. Likewise, if inflation is the focus but investors believe it is declining, both stocks and bonds do well.

When inflation is not on the radar screen and investors focus on economic growth, the assets diverge. If growth looks strong, investors will dump bonds to capture the higher returns from stocks. Should growth appear to be easing, investors will turn to the safety of bonds to avoid a potential decline in stocks.

Correlations among other pairs of assets also change. In the late 1990s, the correlation between the large company index, the S&P 500, and small stock indexes was about 62 percent. In 2006, the correlation changed to 94 percent. Likewise, foreign developed country stocks had a correlation with U.S. stocks of about 40 percent at the start of 2003, but that had changed to around 70 percent in 2006.

The argument made by advocates of CAPM is that these short-term changes in correlations do not matter. Investors should be investing for longer periods, and the long-term correlations will hold despite periods of fluctuation. Investors should be concerned only if correlations using 20 or 30 years of data are changing. Yet, this focus on the very long term does not help an investor achieve goals with an efficient portfolio during those periods of fluctuation. The unfortunate truth is that correlations often rise at times when investors most need diversification to work. When there is stress in the markets or the economy, most asset values tend to decline as investors panic and seek to purchase more short-term Treasury bills or other very low-risk investments. The result is that a supposedly diversified portfolio declines, because all or most of its holdings deviate from their historic correlations and decline at the same time. Sometimes these higher correlations are short-lived, but sometimes higher correlations among assets persist for longer periods.

One way many pension funds and institutional investors deal with changes is to review the asset allocation every three to five years. Here, investors identify which assets they want to consider for their portfolios and rerun the optimizers. This process was thought to be sufficient to discover true long-term changes in the investment markets without trapping the investors into making changes because of short-term market changes called *noise*. The infrequent reviews and the use of long-term data usually resulted only in minor portfolio changes. Even the periodic reviews still left the investors invested heavily in equities during bear markets.

The markets are not as efficient as theory contends. If they were, the data and the results would not fluctuate as much as they do. Unfortunately, investors who rely on the notion that markets are highly efficient and thereby use historic data take the risk that the markets are about to make one of their secular changes and that the change will be adverse to the investors' interests for a decade or more.

## WHAT IS RISK?

Investment risk under both MPT and CAPM is defined as the standard deviation, or volatility, of investment returns. That means the risk of a portfolio or asset is considered to be the amount by which its price fluctuates over time. It doesn't matter if the fluctuation is upward or downward or how long each up or down trend lasts.

For most investors, however, risk is something else. Risk for most investors is the possibility that the portfolio won't achieve the investor's goals within the investor's time horizon, such as paying for retirement and having enough assets to leave something for heirs or charity. Under this definition of risk, an asset could have low volatility and still be very risky to an investor. Or an investment could have very high short-term volatility and still not present a great risk that the investor will not meet his or her goals.

## Real World Risks

A good definition of investment risk is something along this line: "not knowing the future of the world," which I heard Peter Bernstein use in a speech. The real world risk for most investors is not a statistic such as standard deviation or variance. To most investors, risk is the probability that they will outlive their money or, put another way, that their assets won't be able to deliver the after-inflation income needed to meet their spending needs and goals. For some, a shorter-term risk is that they won't be able to pay for their children's education.

Another risk is that there is an extended bull market such as the one that began in 1982, but the investor misses much of it by holding a well-diversified portfolio or a low-risk portfolio instead of owning a high percentage of stocks. Risk also could mean earning lower returns than would be earned by putting money in a riskless investment, such as treasury bills. Different investors will have different attitudes towards risk and different definitions of risk—and CAPM does not include any of them.

One problem from the perspective of advocates of CAPM is that most of the risks listed cannot be measured. In addition, periodically unusual or anomalous events occur that cannot be captured in statistics, such as the widespread market meltdown that occurred after the collapse of Long-Term Capital Management in 1998. An investor cannot know when these events will occur or what will trigger them, but he can be sure that such events will occur in his investment lifetime.

An attempt to resolve the risk issue is to add another step to the creation of the efficient portfolio. This step became fairly widespread among institutional investors and investment professionals after 2000. Once the efficient portfolio is identified, it is subject to a computation known as Monte Carlo simulation. This is a mathematic technique originally used in the development of nuclear weapons.

A Monte Carlo simulation involves using either historic market data or randomly generated returns that are based on historic data. The portfolio's performance is analyzed over a large number of possible scenarios or outcomes. Usually, at least 500 different scenarios are calculated. With today's computer hardware and software this can be done in a minute or less. In the simulation, the returns of the portfolio over each scenario are calculated, and it is determined whether or not the investor would have met his goals in that scenario. The same process is undertaken for 499 additional scenarios.

The software calculates the number of scenarios in which the portfolio met the goals of the investor. The answer is given as a probability. For example, the portfolio met the goal in 85 percent of the scenarios tested. So, the result is that there is an 85 percent probability that the portfolio will meet the investor's goals.

There are critics of Monte Carlo simulations, just as there are critics of CAPM. Foremost among the criticisms is that the probability number can give an investor false confidence. An 85 percent probability of success means there is a 15 percent probability of failure. The simulation also cannot give the probability that the investor will live through a period of failure. If the investor retires at the start of an extended or severe bear market, there could be a 100 percent probability that the portfolio will fail to meet its goals. Monte Carlo simulations are an improvement, because they take an investor away from the notion that there is one possible result from the efficient portfolio. A Monte Carlo simulation also allows for the possibility that there will be a "once-in-a-lifetime event" in the markets that adversely affects an investor's portfolio. If the simulation helps the investor recognize this possibility, it also might cause the investor to adjust the portfolio to reduce the potential harm from such an event. The simulations still can give an investor a false impression or focus attention on the wrong factors.

## THE DARK SIDE OF INDEX FUNDS

Though one need not invest solely in index funds to follow CAPM, most advocates of CAPM recommend investing in index funds instead of actively managed accounts and mutual funds.

A rich body of research backs the preference for index funds. Numerous studies have concluded that a minority of mutual funds earn returns exceeding those of the market indexes over long periods of time. The general conclusion is that a broad-based market index earns higher returns than about two thirds of mutual funds. Therefore, an investor is likely to earn higher returns by selecting an index fund than by trying to identify a money manager who will add alpha by earning more than the index.

Several explanations are advanced to explain the superiority of index funds, and these were discussed earlier in this chapter. More detailed arguments and evidence can be found in *A Random Walk Down Wall Street: The Time-Tested Strategy for Successful Investing* by Burton G. Malkiel (New York: W. W. Norton, 1973, 2007) and books by John Bogle, such as *Bogle on Mutual Funds: New Perspectives for the Intelligent Investor* (New York: Dell, 1994) and *Common Sense on Mutual Funds: New Imperatives for the Intelligent Investor* (New York: John Wiley & Sons, 1999). The evidence also is presented in *Capital Ideas: The Improbable Origins of Modern Wall Street* by Peter L. Bernstein (Hoboken, NJ: John Wiley & Sons, 2005). But there are arguments made against index investing.

Most stock indexes are capitalization weighted. That means a stock's weight in the index is determined by its market capitalization, or the number of shares outstanding multiplied by the share price. The larger a company's capitalization, the larger is its weight in the index. The largest companies have the greatest weight in the index and the greatest influence on the performance of the index. The largest-capitalization stocks in the index essentially determine the return of the index. In the S&P 500, for example, the 50 largest capitalization stocks determine the index's behavior, while the smallest 450 stocks have almost no influence on the returns earned by investors in the index.

For example, in mid-2006 ExxonMobil comprised 3.15 percent of the S&P 500, and General Electric was 3.08 percent. Rounding out the top 10 stocks were Microsoft, Citigroup, Bank of America, Procter & Gamble, Pfizer, Johnson & Johnson, American International Group, and Altria Group. Together, these 10 stocks accounted for 19.45 percent of the index. At the bottom of the portfolio were stocks that each accounted for 0.01 percent of the index each, including: Maytag, Cooper Tire & Rubber, Nicor, Navistar International, Big Lots, Dillards, Peoples Energy, Hercules, Dynegy, and Applied Micro Circuits. A little over 20 percent of the index was in information economy (technology) stocks, and 46.4 percent was in service economy stocks.

These weights have changed dramatically over time. In the early 1980s after oil prices rose for most of the prior decade and oil company stocks rose along with them, energy companies accounted for about 20 percent of the index. In the late 1990s, technology stocks were over 20 percent of the index at their peak. By 2006, the top 10 stocks listed above were more diverse than the top 10 in the late 1990s.

These wide variations are the result of the capitalization weighting of the major indexes and lead to problems for investors.

## Is Bigger Better?

A stock's capitalization is its price multiplied by the number of shares outstanding. Companies that are large in other ways (revenues, earnings) tend to have the highest stock capitalizations, so major indexes are weighted toward large companies. In addition, a stock's capitalization increases as its price increases. The more a stock price rises relative to other stock prices, the greater the stock's share of the index becomes. The index fund has to buy more of the stock as the price rises.

The result at market turning points is the stocks that have the highest valuations and have had the greatest returns in the recent past comprise the greatest share of the index and of index funds. The index fund was forced to buy more of these stocks as their values increased, though these are the stocks most likely to either fall or have below average returns in coming years. In other words, an index fund is required to buy at high prices and sell at low prices. This is the opposite of what most successful advisors advise.

In a bull market, the capitalization weighting can be an advantage. The index fund essentially is engaged in momentum investing. It is buying more of the stocks that are rising the fastest. But after a market peak, whether it is an overall peak or a peak in the sectors with the best recent performance, those often are the stocks that fall the most. Capitalization weighting increases losses in market declines. That is why in the post-1999 bear market the average mutual fund outperformed the S&P 500 Index.

To an investor who can withstand extended and large bear market losses, index investing will be profitable over the long term. But many investors cannot absorb the extreme bear market losses that are generated by capitalization-weighted indexes and would be better served by other portfolios. For example, studies have shown that an equal weight index (one that gives an equal weight to each stock in the index) earns higher returns than a capitalization-weighted index over the long term and also is less volatile.

As indexing became popular and indexes were developed for assets other than U.S. stocks, similar disadvantages of their weighting methods were encountered.

The most popular index for international stock investors is the Morgan Stanley Capital International Europe, Australia and Far East Index, known as MSCI EAFE or simply EAFE. This index covers 21 countries and about 1,200 common stocks. It is considered the most efficient way to invest in the developed stock markets of the world. Emerging market stocks are in other indexes.

EAFE is constructed by first determining each country's stock market weighting according to the relative size, or capitalization, of each country's stock market. Because stock markets do not have the same rate of return each year, the actual weightings vary over time with the relative performances of the different stock indexes. The stock markets with the largest capitalization are the greatest share of the index. For much of the 1980s, Japan accounted for about 60 percent of the index. Its influence in the index declined during the country's bear market after 1989. More recently, Japan and the United Kingdom combined accounted for about 49 percent of EAFE.

By investing in an EAFE index fund, an investor essentially is making a significant bet on Japan's stock market. In the 1980s this was a good bet. In the 1990s, this was a losing bet because Japan was in an extended bear market.

After the country weightings are determined, an index is constructed for each country. The country indexes use capitalization, just as most major U.S. stock indexes do. In addition, a stock must meet certain requirements for liquidity, free float of shares, and other factors to be included in the index. In a number of countries, a relatively small number of stocks qualify for the index and literally a handful or fewer companies determine the returns of many of the country indexes within EAFE.

## Managing Indexes

Contrary to what many investors believe, market indexes are not a natural creation. Indexes often are referred to as "the market," and many investors treat indexes as though they are determined by market or other impersonal forces. In fact, the indexes are constructed by people and adjusted by people. The Standard & Poor's 500, the most popular index, is constructed by a committee of nine people. The committee meets regularly and decides which stocks should be added to and deleted from the index. Some stocks are deleted by actions outside of the committee's control, such as mergers and bankruptcies. The other changes are made by the committee. The committee determines the industry weightings in the index, the number of stocks in each industry, and the specific stocks. The S&P 500, along with other indexes, essentially is a managed portfolio. It apparently is managed well enough that it earns higher returns than most mutual funds, but it is managed.

The same is true of most other market indexes. The securities in the index are determined either by the judgments of people or by numerical criteria established by people. There is nothing necessarily wrong with this. Yet many investors are under the impression that a market index is determined by some natural process. Instead it is created by people and their judgments just as actively managed mutual fund portfolios are.

In addition, firms that create market indexes earn fees from mutual funds and other investment firms that invest according to those indexes.

As index funds gained popularity, more firms became interested in developing indexes and convincing money managers to establish funds that follow their indexes. The result is that index creators compete for business. This gives index developers an incentive to develop indexes that earn higher returns and take more risk to earn those returns instead of indexes that simply reflect the stock markets. It probably is not a coincidence that the number of changes made in some indexes increased during the 1990s as interest in index funds surged.

The changes in the indexes also create problems for investors.

Additions to and subtractions from the indexes are known in advance. Some index creators use published formulas, so investors are able to determine the changes before they are officially announced. Other index firms announce the changes after the firm determines them but before they are implemented. In either case, index fund managers must buy and sell the stocks and must try to do so in ways that do not reduce their returns or affect the market. They must decide when to make the transactions and whether to use futures and options to hedge against market changes during the transition period. At the same time, there are stock arbitrageurs who try to profit from the announced changes and the moves they know index fund managers must make. The arbitrageurs buy in advance the stocks the index funds will have to buy and sell short those the index funds will have to sell.

Studies of the effect of index changes indicate that index funds lose value relative to the published indexes because of this process. Honghui Chen, Gregory Noronha, CFA, and Vijay Singal, CFA, in "Index Changes and Losses to Index Fund Investors" (*Financial Analysts Journal*, July/August 2006) estimated that collectively index fund investors lose about $2 billion from the changes. That does not mean that index investors lose this amount relative to non-index investors. The losses are from the cost of making the change transactions and from the exaggerated moves in stock prices caused by the changes. The study demonstrates that there are inefficiencies in index investing.

One study, "Long-Term Returns on the Original S&P 500 Companies" by Jeremy J. Siegel and Jeremy D. Schwartz (*Financial Analysts Journal*, January/February 2006), concluded that changes in the indexes might not be profitable for investors. Siegel and Schwartz also concluded that simply buying and holding the original companies in the S&P 500 Index in March 1957 would have generated higher returns by 2006 than investing in the updated index over the years.

A very strong argument against index funds is mutual fund behemoth Dimensional Fund Advisors, or DFA. Most investors are not aware of the company, because it accepts investments only from institutional investors and from clients of money managers or financial advisors who have taken education sessions from DFA.

In 25 years, DFA has accumulated over $100 billion in assets under management, and its funds consistently beat their designated market indexes. DFA is advised by academics Kenneth French and Eugene Fama. Fama is the developer of the Efficient Market Hypothesis discussed earlier in this chapter. The DFA view is that capitalization weighting of the indexes is their weakness. DFA's research shows that tilting a portfolio toward smaller stocks and value-priced stocks earns higher returns than buying the indexes. DFA offers funds that use mechanical formulas to buy portfolios that tweak their respective indexes toward smaller and value-priced stocks. Though the funds are considered actively managed, they charge very low fees, a little above index fund fees.

Some critics say that skewing a portfolio to smaller company stocks increases returns only by increasing volatility and risk. In response, DFA has started new funds that add more large company stocks to its usual collection of small company stocks. It says that the result will be above-index returns with less volatility than its traditional funds.

## TRUE DIVERSIFICATION

An efficient portfolio is supposed to be diversified. A properly diversified portfolio will have less risk than a *non*efficient portfolio with the same rate of return.

In practice, however, most efficient portfolios generated by portfolio optimizers are heavily weighed toward equities or assets that are highly correlated with equities. The portfolios appear to be diversified because different types of equities are involved: Large-cap U.S. equities, small-cap U.S. equities, emerging market stocks, developed country international stocks, and private equity, among other possibilities. While their correlations with each other are less than 100 percent, the correlations are fairly high. As discussed earlier, the correlations increase at times, especially at times when an investor wants assets in the portfolio to have low correlations with each other.

This lack of true diversification is partly due to the lack of data. U.S. stocks and some developed overseas stock markets are the assets for which the most historic data is available. For other types of assets, less data is available and that data is not as reliable or detailed as the stock data. An investor who wants to use CAPM to develop an efficient portfolio is limited to asset classes for which enough data is available.

The low diversification also might be because the data show equities to have the highest long-term returns. CAPM assumes the investor can and will hold for the very long term the fixed portfolio with the highest long-term return for a given level of risk. An investor who seeks relatively high long-term returns will hold a portfolio heavily-weighted toward equities. Different types of equities will be mixed in the portfolio to reduce correlations and risk a bit.

For whatever reason, in practice many policy portfolios are not diversified enough to protect investors from the effects of an extended bear market in equities.

# THE ANTI-CAPM CACOPHONY

Though CAPM is widely used, criticisms of it are significant and becoming more widespread. Individuals who have successfully managed money for decades tend to be critical of CAPM. Warren Buffett has discussed the deficiencies of CAPM in some of his annual reports, which are available on the Berkshire Hathaway web site (www.berkshirehathaway.com).

Another strong critic is Martin Whitman of the Third Avenue funds, and those criticisms often find their way into his shareholder letters. In his firm's semiannual Letter to Our Shareholders dated April 30, 2003, Whitman unfavorably compared CAPM's theories to the way he and his firm analyze companies and buy stocks. It and other letters are available on the fund's web site (www.thirdavenuefunds. com). After restating a couple of the principles of CAPM (which he calls *MCT*, for Modern Capital Theory), Whitman writes, "These MCT views are utterly naïve." Elsewhere, Whitman concludes, "Much of MCT is based on utterly unrealistic views of the real world." Whitman's conclusion is: "I remain convinced that over the long term, an investment in TAVF [the ticker symbol for Third Avenue Value Fund] will combine both greater upside potential, and much less downside risk, than would an investment in an Index Fund such as Vanguard 500 Index Fund."

Harry Markowitz made explicit criticisms of CAPM in "Market Efficiency: A Theoretical Distinction and So What?" (*Financial Analysts Journal,* September 2005), stating that CAPM is dependent on three assumptions that do not reflect the real world. While Markowitz believes two of the assumptions are fairly harmless, he believes the third is not. In its purest form, CAPM states there is just one efficient portfolio, and every investor should own it. Since investors have different levels of risk aversion, they adjust this portfolio to increase or reduce risk. Risk-averse investors add cash, and risk takers add leverage. CAPM assumes that each investor has unlimited ability to sell assets short and leverage the portfolio at the risk-free interest rate. These practices allow every investor to move along the same efficient frontier curve.

This is not how CAPM works in practice because the assumption is not valid. Instead, investors who can take more risk or who need a higher return add riskier (or more volatile) assets to their portfolios. Investors with low risk tolerances hold more cash and short-term U.S. Treasury securities. In Markowitz's view, this practice is exactly what portfolio managers were doing before CAPM and what he captured in his writing on MPT.

Sometimes actions speak louder than words. A predecessor of today's Barclays Global Investors was the innovator in index investing, and BGI now manages more than $1 trillion in index-based portfolios. The firm manages more assets in index strategies than any other manager.

Yet for years BGI has been building up another aspect of its business directed at institutional investors. After establishing itself as the premier index investor, BGI recruited a number of finance and economics academics along with Ph.D. holders in various scientific and mathematical fields to apply their quantitative skills to investing. At first it focused these efforts on tactical asset allocation, an effort to increase returns by periodically switching the allocation of portfolios between different types of assets, such as stock index funds and bond index funds. Then, BGI turned its attention to active management, seeking quantitative ways to exceed the returns of an index while incurring less risk. The team initially focused on U.S. stock indexes, studying data to learn which factors could be used to adjust a portfolio of stocks to achieve a higher return with less risk. After successfully building this "alpha tilts" business, BGI moved on to other active, mathematics-based strategies. It developed a hedge fund–like business of investment strategies with the goals of achieving returns similar to a stock index with less volatility than a stock index and very low correlation to the stock index. All these active strategies now are a major part of BGI's business. The hedge fund operation alone has about $370 billion in assets.

## FIXING CAPM

Others are attempting to refine or improve CAPM rather than tossing it out.

Jeremy Siegel, author of *Stocks for the Long Run* (New York: McGraw-Hill, 1998), and retired hedge fund manager Michael Steinhardt joined Wisdom Tree Investments to help market new exchange-traded index funds. These funds weight stocks according to dividend yields rather than market capitalization. Siegel's review of historic data indicates that dividend-weighted portfolios would have earned higher returns than capitalization-weighted indexes, with much lower losses in bear markets.

Robert Arnott likewise reviewed historic data and determined that what he calls fundamentally weighted indexes earned higher returns with less risk than capitalization-weighted indexes. Arnott weights stocks using factors such as book value, trailing five-year average cash flows, and revenues. Others suggest weighting a portfolio in favor of smaller capitalizations and low price-to-book values instead of capitalization. Rydex Funds offers an equal-weighted S&P 500 Index Fund. This fund owns all the stocks that are in the S&P 500 Index, but each stock is equally weighted instead of being weighted by capitalization.

Most of these alternative index methods actually are not indexing. Almost all use the traditional strategies of value investors to find stocks selling at lower valuations than the capitalization-weighted market indexes. Value investing has its good times and bad times but over the long term has earned higher returns than growth stock or index investing. In addition, value investing has less risk than index investing using almost any measure of risk.

These alternative "indexes" were developed using "back testing." That is when past data are used to determine what returns would have been if an investor had used a particular strategy. But back testing is notorious for not working once the results are well known and investors try to implement the strategy in practice and real time. We discuss that in more detail in Chapter 6 when we review data mining.

Another attempt to fix CAPM is to develop different optimizers. Users of optimizers learn that they have to use constraints based on their own assessments of likely market outcomes. Otherwise, an unconstrained optimizer will develop an efficient portfolio that makes the investor uncomfortable and relies heavily on past events that are not likely to be repeated in the near future. One firm, New Frontier Advisors LLC, developed an optimizer that does not generate one efficient frontier and efficient portfolio. Instead, the optimizer calculates the average of hundreds of efficient frontiers using Monte Carlo simulation. The firm believes that the efficient portfolio from this process is more diversified and more stable than those from traditional optimizers.

Even strong proponents of and developers of the Efficient Market Hypothesis and CAPM have wavered a bit in recent years. The latest editions of Burton Malkiel's *A Random Walk Down Wall Street* admit that there are strategies that seem to effectively beat the market indexes. These strategies are known as anomalies in the EMH. Its developer, Eugene Fama, surprised some observers in recent years. He said that he never was a proponent of the "strong form" of the hypothesis, which argued that the markets were perfectly efficient and prices immediately reflected all available information, even nonpublic information. Fama said poorly informed investors could make bad decisions that distort market prices and make the markets somewhat irrational for a period of time.

Finally, William Sharpe weighed in by revamping his CAPM model in a 2006 book, *Investors and Markets: Portfolio Choices, Asset Prices and Investment Advice* (Princeton: Princeton University Press, 2006). Sharpe believes his new approach is a better way to teach students how portfolios are constructed and securities are priced.

Sharpe's new approach drops mean-variance analysis in favor of a simulation known as the *state/preference approach*. Sharpe now believes that the simplification used to develop CAPM was an over-simplification. The state/preference model does not assume that investment returns have a normal statistical distribution. Instead, it recognizes that extreme returns occur more often than is the case in a normal distribution. In addition, the calculations in the state/preference model are easier.

The initial reviews of Sharpe's new approach state that the new model is an easier way for students to understand how markets set the prices of investments. The new model shows that it is rational for investors to consider nonmarket risks in making decisions and discards the notion that all investors have the same beliefs about the markets and can have only one rational conclusion. Yet it still requires a significant amount of calculations, and state/preference theory is not provable—and, as Markowitz recently opined, "I find [the state/preference approach uses] a very general set of assumptions out of which very little specific can be deducted"(quoted in Joel Chernoff, "Rethinking CAPM," *Pensions & Investments,* 2 October 2006). The initial consensus seems to be that while the new approach will be helpful to students, it is unlikely to be something investors can use to develop portfolios.

## WHAT MATTERS MOST

CAPM fails to meet the needs of most investors. If the key invest-ment years of an investor's lifetime coincide with a bull market in equities, following CAPM will be beneficial. In other periods, investors can be harmed by using CAPM, at least as most people practice it. The reliance on long-term data puts investors at peril, because there are periods that will differ drastically from the long-term averages. Returns, risk, correlations, and other factors change over time.

Most investors should be concerned with investment performance for the next 10 years or so, not over the past 70 or 80 years. Investors know that there will be bull and bear markets. They cannot afford to see all or a portion of their portfolios decline by 50 percent or more in a bear market, as happens about once every generation. They also do not want to miss a high percentage of the returns of a bull market.

The biggest risk to most investors is the valuation cycle of equities and other investments. The traditional theories of investment advice do not manage this risk. CAPM says such a risk either does not exist or cannot be managed. Fortunately, alternatives to CAPM have been developed. These developments incorporate the actual practices of successful money managers and account for the risks and shortcomings of CAPM. These enhancements are better suited for most individual investors. The alternatives also require the investor to have more of the characteristics of a fox than a hedgehog. We discuss these enhancements to investing and how to use them to develop a portfolio strategy in the next few chapters.

# CHAPTER 4

## HOW FOXES LOOK
## AT MARKETS

Investment management substantially improved with the reception of ideas that flowed from the academic world during the last five decades. Investors learned to focus on risk as well as potential returns, that risk can be reduced by diversification, and that effective diversification means the return patterns of the assets in a portfolio should not be highly correlated with each other. Academic studies revealed that a large percentage of mutual funds and money managers fail to earn higher returns than a market index. These studies taught investors to tell the difference between a manager with skill who generates alpha and one who simply takes more risk than an index and earns higher returns in a bull market by generating beta.

Yet, the investment advice drawn from the academic studies did not meet the needs of most investors. The Efficient Market Hypothesis (EMH) that underlies much of the advice is not reflective of real-world investment markets. Users of the Capital Asset Pricing Model (CAPM), which builds on EMH, found that the characteristics of assets—such as returns, volatility, and correlations—change over time and can differ markedly from their long-term averages in any period less than the long term. That makes the efficient portfolio a moving target.

## A LOOK AT REAL MARKETS

Experience shows that CAPM achieves an investor's goals only over the very long term or in equity bull markets. EMH does not acknowledge the possibility of long-term bull markets and bear markets with returns significantly higher or lower than the long-term average. Yet there are few calendar years in which the returns for the major stock market indexes are close to the long-term average.

From 1901 to 2005, the Dow Jones Industrial Average lost 10 percent or more in a calendar year 21 percent of the time. The Dow returned 10 percent or more in a calendar year 48 percent of the time. And 31 percent of the time the Dow's return for a calendar year was between positive 10 percent and negative 10 percent.

More importantly, the positive and negative years do not appear to be random. Instead, positive years tend to cluster and form long-term, or secular, bull markets; negative years tend to cluster and form secular bear markets. From 1942 through 1965, the Dow was in a 24-year bull market; only 25 percent of the years had negative returns, and the total return for the period was 774 percent. From 1966 through 1981 the tables turned. Those 16 years were a bear market in which the Dow had negative returns for 44 percent of the calendar years. The return of the Dow for that period was negative 10 percent. This was followed by the greatest bull market in history, the 18 years from 1982 through 1999. The Dow had positive returns 89 percent of the years for a return of 1,214 percent.

The average return over 70 years or longer is of little value to most investors. The risk and return for the next 10 years are their main concerns. If the stock market indexes are in a bear market for most of the first 10 years of an individual's retirement, for example, the individual is not likely to have enough capital to meet the income and spending goals of retirement.

Clearly, the investment markets are not as efficient as hypothesized in CAPM, and the differences are significant to individual investors who must invest during their lifetimes, not the long term.

The shortcomings in CAPM are evident in the significant movement of investors away from the strategy since 1999. Following the peaks in the stock market indexes in 2000, institutional investors and wealthy individuals began shifting large sums of money into hedge funds. These lightly regulated investment vehicles operate contrary to the foundations of CAPM. The managers of these funds assume that at least portions of the investment markets are inefficient and that those inefficiencies can be identified often enough to generate alpha, or risk-adjusted excess returns, greater than those of the indexes.

Peter Bernstein, consultant to institutional investors, author of *Capital Ideas* (Hoboken, NJ: John Wiley & Sons, 2005) and longtime advocate of CAPM and index funds, modified his views in late 2002 and early 2003. He initially recommended that pension funds and other institutional investors abandon the policy portfolio. Bernstein started advocating a different approach to investing that involved hedging against different possible investment outcomes and hoping for a fairly modest long term return with low volatility. He subsequently modified these views, as we will see in a later chapter.

Institutional investors also began to move away from a longtime practice of reviewing their investment allocations only every three to five years. Under CAPM, these periodic reviews were deemed sufficient because investors were focused on the long term, and the fundamentals of the asset classes and their relationships to each other were believed not to make meaningful changes over shorter periods. Experience in the 1990s and early 2000s taught investment managers that the short-term changes can be significant enough to disrupt progress toward long-term goals. Many funds decided that more frequent reviews and portfolio adjustments were necessary.

Advisers to individual investors also began seeking alternatives to CAPM. The May 2003 issue of *Bloomberg Wealth Manager* interviewed a number of financial planners and money managers who were abandoning CAPM and adopting other investment approaches.

The answer for investors is not to completely abandon the foundations of MPT and CAPM. Instead, investors should take the elements of these theories that are valid and build on them with new theories that better explain how markets work and point to strategies that will result in a better investment experience. Specifically, there are issues with CAPM that need to be resolved:

- Why are asset prices more volatile than the underlying fundamentals of the assets?
- If the markets were as described in Efficient Market Hypothesis, the long-term risk-free rate of return on cash investments would be much higher than it actually is, and the return premium for investing in equities would be much lower. There would be little extra return from investing in equities, because there would be little extra risk. This is known as the "equity premium puzzle," with the higher long-term return generated by stocks over cash and other investments being the equity premium.
- Why do stock prices change without a corresponding change in fundamentals, such as the growth rate of earnings or dividends?

## FINDING RATIONALITY IN IRRATIONAL MARKETS

*Rational expectations* is a label for the theory underlying the Efficient Market Hypothesis. It holds that investors know all the relevant information about the markets, they interpret it the same way, and they interpret the information accurately. The actions of investors cannot contribute to the volatility of the markets, and financial risks cannot come from the economy. Risks and volatility arise from outside the economy and markets.

Rational Expectations Theory and CAPM assume everyone acts rationally all the time, processes information instantly, and interprets it accurately. All this processing makes the markets efficient, so no one can earn a return higher than the market indexes either by smart stock picking, good market timing, or other investment methods, without taking more risk than the index. The appropriate way to invest under Rational Expectations is to choose a long-term allocation, fill it with index funds, and hold the portfolio for the long term.

We know from common sense and experience that some of the underlying assumptions of Rational Expectations and CAPM do not reflect the markets. If markets were always efficient and rational, there would not be wide price swings in either different asset classes or in different securities. There also would be no long-term benefit from investing in stocks instead of other assets. Stocks would have the same long-term return as treasury bills, because there would be no additional risk in stocks. The standard response for inaccurate assumptions is that they make building a model and analyzing the problem easier, and the assumptions are neutral. They do not affect the validity of the model or its results. While this might be true of CAPM's assumptions regarding the very long-term behavior of the markets, it clearly is not true in the shorter periods in which most investors live and must achieve their goals.

A more realistic explanation of the markets, and one that provides more useful advice to investors, is *Rational Beliefs*. Its primary developer and proponent is Mordecai Kurz, of the economics faculty of Stanford University. Rational Beliefs corrects many of the problems in CAPM and EMH. It does a better job of building on the original Modern Portfolio Theory and recognizes and explains what I call the Valuation Cycle and Kurz calls *investment regimes*, to which all investment assets are subject. I believe it also explains the strategies used by many successful investment managers and shows investors how they can earn higher returns with lower risk. Rational Beliefs Theory should make investors realize that managing valuation cycles is the cornerstone of successful investing.

A capsule explanation of the typical valuation cycle for an investment asset is as follows. An investment will be at a low price for a period of time, essentially ignored by investors. Gradually, it will attract the attention of a few investors. Its price will increase. As the price increases and early investors reap profits, the profits attract more investors. The fundamentals of the asset might improve, also making the asset even more attractive. The rising investment demand for the asset pushes the price still higher. At some point, the price rises faster than the fundamentals of the asset. That increases the valuation, whether value is determined by the price-earnings ratio of a stock or some other measure. Eventually, the price soars far above its cycle low, and the valuation is far higher than it was at the low point and than the long-term average. Then, the process reverses. Investors start to sell the asset, and the price begins to decline. As the price declines, more investors sell and push the price lower. Investors seek greener pastures, and the price slides back to a low level and a low valuation.

Rational Beliefs explains why this cycle happens.

## FUNDAMENTALS OF RATIONAL BELIEFS

CAPM teaches that all investors are rational, right, and in agreement all the time. Rational Beliefs says all investors are rational but not necessarily correct or in agreement. Each investor has his or her own theory about which investment regime is the current one, how long it will last, and what the next regime will be. Some investors are always bearish; some are always bullish; most investors swing between the two. Each investor selects investments based on his or her outlook and the expected risk-adjusted returns that lead from that outlook. While investors will process all the information they receive, all will not interpret it the same way or correctly.

Rational Beliefs also asserts that investors' beliefs are dynamic. Investors can disagree, and individual investors can change their beliefs over time. Changes in the beliefs of investors are the foundation of market fluctuations and cycles.

Economic and investment variables have long-term averages or normal ranges. For example, stocks have a long-term average annual rate of return, standard deviation or variance, price-earnings ratio, and other characteristics. Interest rates, economic growth rates, productivity, and other factors of the economy also have known long-term characteristics. Technology and other factors can change these characteristics for periods of time, but the long-term nature of these factors and the true structure of the economy are available to all investors.

Because the economy and markets are not stationary or fixed during any particular time period, the behavior of an economic variable or an investment can differ from its long-term, normal range. The change can be due to technology, organizational structure, or other factors. Each period of change is called a *regime* by Kurz. Within a long-term regime, there can be short-term or *subregimes*. In conventional investment terminology, there are secular or long-term bull and bear markets, and within them cyclical or short-term bull and bear markets. The structure of the economy and markets will be relatively fixed for most of a regime.

Investors do not know exactly how changes in technology and other factors will affect the economy and markets and do not know how the markets and economy will move from their present state to the long-term normal range. The scope of the changes during that journey also is unknown. It is easy to look back and identify the different investment regimes or cycles for each investment. But while the markets are operating under these regimes, no one knows the beginning or ending dates of a regime or the data it will generate. Even an investor who discovers the parameters of a regime—and of the next regime—cannot be certain that forecast is accurate and will act with a degree of uncertainty.

Though investors cannot know the route the markets will take, they must make investment decisions. To make these decisions, they form their own theories and forecasts and they use models to guide their decisions. Investors can disagree in both their theories and their forecasts, and they and their models can also disagree over the interpretation of new information and data.

Investors have access to history and past data, and they use these tools to develop theories and models about the markets and investment strategies. The conclusions and forecasts investors develop are rational beliefs. A rational belief is one that cannot be contradicted by the available data about market activity. Two or more investors can develop different and contradictory theories that are not contradicted by the available evidence. They are acting rationally though they disagree. The investors agree about the long-term results from the markets but disagree about the lessons learned from their study and their strategies for investing today.

An investor who chooses to follow CAPM can be rational because it is rational for an investor to build a portfolio and strategy around the long-term averages. That investor might believe that structural changes do not occur, will not occur while he is investing, or might occur but will not have an effect on the ultimate returns for the relevant period.

The investors who do not follow CAPM also are rational. They do not disagree about what happened in the past, but they do have different views of the future. These investors conclude that while today's markets and economy are similar to the past, there also are differences. They use past statistics or descriptions of current financial conditions or both to fashion theories about the future and strategies to profit from the theories. Though they are studying the same history and data, these investors will not agree with each other. Between them, these investors formulate many different theories and strategies, and many of these approaches contradict each other. Each investor is behaving rationally as long as the belief cannot be contradicted by the known data. Because of their different theories, strategies, and models, the investors also have different opinions about how to respond to new information.

Investment markets are complex and volatile because society and the economy undergo structural changes. In the face of such changes, investors can decide that the past alone is not a sufficient basis for assessing future risks. For example, an investor can decide that the future might be similar to the past but different enough that it is appropriate to construct a portfolio that differs somewhat from the one that had the best risk and return trade-off over the long term. Or an investor can decide that the future will be very different from the past and that a portfolio very different from that indicated by the long-term averages is appropriate.

The changes in the economy and society can cause investors' beliefs to differ in three ways. Investors can disagree about the nature of the changes, the intensity of those changes, and the timing of the changes. As new information is received, investors can form different opinions about the significance of that information and how it will affect the markets.

Not surprisingly, the way an investor assesses risk under Rational Beliefs is not the volatility or standard deviation of an investment. Risk also is not measured by the past covariances of investments. Rational Beliefs recognizes that in a market investors employ different models in a search for excess returns. The risk an investor faces, according to Kurz, is that he is using an investment model without statistically reliable evidence to verify the underlying theory of the model. Though risk is assessed by continuously interpreting information as it is learned, there simply is insufficient evidence to have a high level of statistical reliability that a model and its conclusions are accurate. Investors can make mistakes, and they know it.

## DYNAMICS OF DISAGREEMENTS

The extent and intensity of the disagreements among investors vary over time, and those variations cause market volatility and cycles. Some investors adopt the long-term averages as their assumptions and invest accordingly, putting them at odds with other investors most of the time. There are groups of investors who are almost always bullish or bearish (that is, optimistic or pessimistic). Most investors reassess their investment outlooks at intervals, using a variety of theories, strategies, and models to evaluate information and adjust their portfolios. Because the mass of investors are using different analytical tools and are regularly reevaluating their outlooks, the range, or state of disagreement between these investors differ over time and move the markets.

Some or even most investors can be wrong at any time. Then they act on these wrong beliefs and turn them into mistakes. The market at any time reflects both the correct actions and the mistaken actions of all investors. Since investors can make mistakes, the market price can be wrong. That is, the market price can differ from what it would be if it were determined by a rational person who had all the relevant information and processed it accurately. This conclusion of Rational Beliefs Theory differs greatly from CAPM and the Efficient Markets Hypothesis.

Here is but one example of how the mistakes of individual investors influence market volatility and cause market prices to be mistaken. A group of investors can develop a theory that an upcoming event is likely to have an adverse effect on the profitability of a company. They sell and push down the stock's price, though no changes have occurred in the company's operations. As time passes, the theory of these investors will be proven or disproved. If the theory was wrong, the stock's price will recover to its original position. An "irrational" move in the stock's price will have occurred because of the mistakes of some investors. Mistakes lead to mispricing in the market.

## BATTLES OF BELIEFS

The dynamic, changing outlooks of investors and the potential for investors to make mistakes are the keys to explaining market volatility and cycles. These changes, the different outlooks of investors, and mistakes are what can cause the level of market volatility to be different from the volatility of underlying fundamentals.

Each investor can be optimistic, pessimistic, or neutral and can change that outlook over time. Since each investor can change, the net levels of optimism and pessimism in a market also can change, and the levels can be measured relative to historic norms. These changes in the relative optimism and pessimism of investors contribute to market volatility over time in several ways.

Based on their theories of the markets and how they interpret developments, investors' market outlooks shift between different degrees of optimism and pessimism. Some investors use models that cause frequent changes, while others alter their outlook less often. The changes and their effects on the markets are what Kurz calls the *dynamics of beliefs*. As individual investors change their outlooks, the ratio of optimists to pessimists in the markets shifts. Kurz calls this ratio of optimists to pessimists the *distribution of beliefs* and argues that changes in this distribution cause market volatility. The changes cause both the secular bull and bear markets, or investment regimes, as well as the cyclical bull and bear markets that occur within secular markets.

When most investors are neutral, rather than optimistic or pessimistic, volatility will be low. News and events will not lead to many changes since most investors were neutral and are likely to interpret new information as reinforcing their neutrality. But if most investors are either optimistic or pessimistic, volatility will be higher. New information is more likely to cause a change in either the intensity of an investor's views or a change in the outlook. For example, when presented with new information, an optimistic investor might become more optimistic or less optimistic or could change to neutral or even pessimistic. Changes along this scale are more likely if the investor has taken a position other than neutral. Therefore, a market is likely to be volatile if most investors were either optimists or pessimists.

Suppose 5 percent of investors are optimists, 5 percent are pessimists, and the other 90 percent are neutral. In this instance, market volatility is likely to be relatively low. New information might induce changes in the positions of the relatively small number of optimists and pessimists but is unlikely to change the positions of the vast majority of investors with neutral outlooks. But if investors are equally divided between optimists and pessimists, market volatility will be higher.

Investors have to make three key decisions to form an investment outlook and to set an investment strategy. These three decisions are potential points of disagreement between or agreement among investors in the market. The first decision is a forecast of the direction of an investment relative to its normal or long-term pattern. The second decision is the interpretation of new information and how it affects the first forecast. The third decision is the intensity with which an investor believes in a decision. Investors might agree on the general direction of an investment but not carry that belief with the same intensity or confidence.

In addition to the distribution of beliefs, another contributor to market volatility is the correlation of beliefs. This is the extent to which the outlooks of investors are the same and shift together in the same direction.

When many investors have similar forecasts and intensity, or a high correlation of beliefs, market volatility is likely to be high. In addition, market prices are likely to be pushed in one direction relative to their fundamental values. When a large percentage of investors are pessimistic, their actions will move prices below what fundamental factors alone would indicate. A large percentage of optimistic investors on the other hand would cause prices to rise above their fundamental values. A high correlation of beliefs among investors causes the extremes of bull markets and bear markets.

The important distributions of belief are consensus and nonconsensus.

In a period of nonconsensus, investors are using widely different models and reaching different forecasts about the markets. Their forecasts and actions tend to offset each other. Market volatility will be low because the optimists and pessimists will serve as counterbalances to each other. It is difficult for the market to establish momentum in one direction or the other.

In a consensus period, investors tend to have similar forecasts and interpret new information in similar ways. Those interpretations tend to reinforce the optimism or pessimism of previous forecasts. As long as this consensus persists, markets will move in the same direction. In a consensus period, market volatility is high. When the consensus is optimistic, the majority of investors buy the same securities; when the consensus is pessimistic, the majority sells the same securities.

Consensus among investors leads to persistence of beliefs, and the persistence of beliefs is the final factor in explaining market cycles or regimes. Kurz argues that a distribution of beliefs among market participants tends to persist. This persistence is due to the widespread modes of communication through which investors tend to interact with and influence each other. Investors generally consult the same sources of information, have access to much of the same data, and select their investment models from among the same universe of choices. Once a distribution of beliefs forms, the communication and information process tends to re-enforce the distribution and make it persistent. Kurz refers to a persistent distribution of beliefs as a *belief regime*. Most investors refer to them as different phases of the market cycles.

## HOW BELIEFS ROIL MARKETS

Rational Beliefs Theory establishes that while investors have the same historic information available to them, they can draw different conclusions from that data. An investor also can change forecasts and swing between optimism and pessimism. Investors are not all-knowing or always right. An investor can make mistakes and take mistaken actions.

The interplay of these actions by different investors dictates current market prices. Because individual investors can make mistakes, a majority of investors collectively can be wrong and push market prices to levels that are not consistent with the underlying economic fundamentals.

Three measures of beliefs in the market are important. The distribution of beliefs among investors determines whether a market generally is optimistic, pessimistic, or neutral. The distribution influences whether prices are above, below, or near the fundamental value of an asset. The distribution also contributes to market volatility. The correlation of beliefs is the extent to which the beliefs and outlooks of investors shift together. A high correlation will lead to market volatility and is a factor in the length of an investment regime or cycle. Finally, the persistence of beliefs also influences the length of a cycle and the extent to which prices can reach an extreme level that deviates from fundamental values.

## The Valuation Cycle

It is the dynamics of investor beliefs that cause market cycles. Figure 4.1 is a tongue-in-cheek view of a market cycle and the changing views of investors during that cycle. As stated in Rational Beliefs Theory, investors range from different degrees of optimism and pessimism during a cycle. We can understand this cycle using Rational Beliefs Theory.

An investment is neglected by investors because it has not had good returns for some time. It has been in a secular, or long-term, bear market. Regardless of what the long-term data for the investment indicate, a majority of investors are pessimistic because returns in recent periods have been below the long-term average.

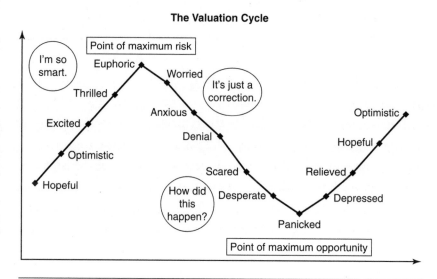

**FIGURE 4.1**   The Valuation Cycle

The fundamental economic factors of the asset also might have been poor. The models most investors use forecast that there will continue to be low returns from the asset for some time. In other words, the distribution of beliefs among investors is predominantly pessimistic and has been for a while; their beliefs are highly correlated and persistent. The market is in a period of extreme pessimism.

A few investors will be attracted to the investment, viewing it as a bargain or seeing some potential for a change of direction. Their unique models cause them to buy. The buying and perhaps other structural changes in the markets or economy increase prices a bit and attract more investors. Over time, as returns for the investment improve or other factors change, more investors become optimistic and add it to their portfolios. The buying will increase returns, attracting more investors. More and more investors become optimistic about the asset and buy it.

The consensus among investors has shifted. At the beginning of the cycle, investors had highly correlated pessimistic beliefs, and those beliefs had persisted. The market gradually moved from that consensus period to a nonconsensus period with both optimists and pessimists, plus many neutral investors. As more investment models cause investors to buy, a new consensus develops. A majority of investors become optimistic, and that optimism is persistent. Eventually, the market turns into the mirror image of the beginning of the cycle. The investment earns high returns for a period of time and many investors become optimistic that such returns will continue. The vast majority of investors become optimistic, and their beliefs are highly correlated and persistent. This was a period of extreme optimism and was the top of the valuation cycle.

After optimism reaches a peak consensus, the process reverses. Over time, optimism decreases and the price declines. This part of the cycle should continue until investors again are predominantly pessimistic.

The length of an investment cycle varies between investments, and there can be lesser cycles within one great cycle. For example, U.S. stocks generally are acknowledged to have had a long-term bear market from 1966 to 1982 and a long-term bull market from 1982 to 1999. Within each of those long periods there were shorter periods in which prices moved counter to the long-term move. In the long bull market, U.S. stocks had significant declines in 1987 and 1991 along with other, smaller declines during the period. Both the secular and cyclical markets are caused by the same process. The difference is one of degree. In a cyclical bear market within a secular bull market, the level of pessimism and consensus of beliefs are not as great as they are during a secular bear market. The pessimism also is not as persistent. Furthermore, the investment models in use during the secular bull market are more likely to interpret new information in an optimistic way than they are in a secular bear market.

Once one accepts the notion that investors can change their minds and make mistakes, it is easy to accept that market prices at any time can differ from the price that would be dictated by financial fundamentals if markets were efficient. After accepting those notions, the two keys to understanding investment cycles are the correlation of beliefs and persistence of beliefs.

Among a population there tend to be a correlations of beliefs and also a persistence of beliefs. A sizeable part of the population tends to adopt the same view most of the time, and once formed those views tend to persist for extended periods. The outlooks and beliefs of the majority change slowly. Once investors fall in love with an investment, it takes a great deal of disappointment for them to turn against the investment. Once investors have been burned in a severe bear market, it takes most of them a long time to forget that and become optimistic about the investment again. (Some analysts use similar theories to explain political cycles.)

It is important for the individual investor to recognize that valuation cycles exist for all investments, and that the cycles are the biggest risk to the individual investor. The key to successful investing is not trying to invest for the long term and to earn the normal long-term return, as CAPM teaches. That long-term return is an average arrived at over many decades. The key for the individual is the pattern of returns that will occur over his investment lifetime. The valuation cycle determines that pattern of returns. Investors should look beyond long-term returns and assess where each investment is in the valuation cycle before deciding how to structure their portfolios.

## HOW BIG AND HOW LONG THE BEAR?

CAPM and some other widely followed investment strategies say to ignore the bear markets and hold stocks and other investments for the long term. The rationale is that the long-term bias for stocks and the economy is positive, and they eventually will return the long-term average to those who continue holding. Bear market losses eventually will turn into bull market gains. That can be sound advice for someone who started investing at the bottom of a bear market or who has a very long investment horizon. Before adopting the long-term outlook, however, investors should consider how long a market decline can last and how steep the losses might be.

Rational Beliefs Theory does not attempt to answer the question of how long either a secular or cyclical trend will last and how wide the variation between the high and low of a cyclical will be. In other words, it does not address how long a correlation of beliefs will persist or how often investors change their forecasts. Those factors depend on the asset involved and the economic circumstances. The most studied asset class is the U.S. stock market, and we can turn to some of the studies for answers to these questions.

One analysis of these questions by John Hussman of the Hussman Funds ("Temporary versus Permanent Returns," *Weekly Market Comment*, 6 October 2006) examined the shorter-term or cyclical moves for U.S. stocks. Hussman reported that the average short-term bull-bear market cycle is close to five years, with stock prices rising 3.75 of these years and declining for 1.25 of those years. He computed the average gain during the bullish period to be 28 percent annualized, or a 152 percent total return, and the average loss during the bearish period to be 28 percent annualized—or 34 percent total. That amounts to a total positive return of 67 percent for the full five-year cycle, on average. The total return for the full cycle is less than half of the peak gains from the bottom of the cycle to its peak. For example, from December 1994 through September 2000 the S&P 500 had a total return of 277 percent. From that point through October 2002, the index lost 46 percent. Over that eight-year cycle, the total return was 104 percent, less than half of the peak return. Over a longer-term cycle, the market still tends to give up about half its peak gains. Hussman calculated that from 1990 through 2000, the S&P 500 returned 536 percent, but the total return from 1990 through October 2002 was 245 percent.

One study of long-term bear markets, by Bryan Taylor of Global Financial Data ("A Century's Lessons," *Bloomberg Personal Finance* December 2002/January 2003), concluded that secular bear markets experience a 75 percent real (after inflation) decline. Taylor concluded that the 75 percent decline pattern held true regardless of how high the bull market returns were, how long the bear market lasted, or what the economic environment was.

An intriguing study of U.S. stock bear markets is *Anatomy of the Bear: Lessons from Wall Street's Four Great Bottoms* by Russell Napier (Hong Kong: CLSA, 2005). Based on a review of markets in 1921,

1932, 1949, and 1982, Napier concluded that bear markets end only when stocks are extremely cheap, which he defines as selling on average at about a 70 percent discount to the replacement cost of net assets. At that time, stocks usually are falling, but trading volume is low. The economy also begins to recover at bear market bottoms. Napier believes that inflation tends to drive down stock valuations to bear market lows, and deflation or the threat of deflation is a sign of bear market bottoms.

The *triple waterfall* concept was developed by Donald Coxe of Harris Investment Management and Jones Howard Investments and is consistent with Rational Beliefs Theory. The typical cycle takes the better part of three decades, according to Coxe. First is the *optimism phase* in which base-building for an asset is followed by strong fundamentals that lead to sustained positive returns. This is followed by even more positive returns as optimism increases to form what Coxe calls *faith* that a New Era has arrived. New investors are drawn into the investment. There is a final peak of the cycle when faith becomes *fanaticism* and finally *mania.*

The positive phase of the investment cycle takes about a decade, according to Coxe. It is followed by about two decades of falling prices that progress from decline to disappointment to despair, giving the name to the Triple Waterfall concept. In the negative period, the investment retraces all or sometimes more than all the appreciation earned in the first decade of positive returns.

No market cycle is exactly like a past market cycle or the average cycle. Some conclusions do emerge from the data. Bear markets, whether cyclical or secular, retrace a significant portion of previous bull market advances. In cyclical bear markets, about half of the bull market gains disappear. In secular bear markets, the losses from bull markets peaks can exceed 50 percent, and in real terms can be 75 percent and more of the bull market gains. Since cyclical bear markets on average last between one and two years, many investors can withstand these losses. Secular bear markets, however, often last a decade or longer. Few investors can stand to have a significant portion of their wealth invested in an asset for the full secular bear market phase of an asset's investment cycle.

## WHAT EVERY INVESTOR SHOULD KNOW

CAPM and MPT provided several key principles for investment success: the concept of diversification, the definition of true diversification, the importance of focusing on risk as well as returns, and the difficulty of achieving true excess returns. As a portfolio strategy, however, they are incomplete. CAPM, in particular, makes assumptions that are benign over the very long term but can be dangerous to investors who must achieve their goals over shorter periods. Rational Beliefs builds on MPT and CAPM by recognizing and explaining the reality of market cycles. Rational Beliefs provides additional key principles investors should use to develop their portfolios.

While long-term data such as returns and correlations are important, investors should know that there will be periods during which results differ greatly from the long-term averages. There is an explanation for why such periods occur, and investors can use that explanation to help identify approximately where an investment is in its valuation cycle. That information can help an investor avoid investing in an asset during an extended period of below average returns.

An investor, especially a retiree or preretiree, should be concerned about investment returns for the next 10 years or so, not the average return over the past 70 years or more. The investor should be alert for structural changes in the markets, the economy, or both. An investor also should try to determine the current regime that comprises the correlation of investor beliefs, the distribution of optimism and pessimism in those beliefs, and how long those beliefs have persisted.

The real risk for investors is not the volatility of an investment. The risk for most investors is failing to achieve their cash flow goals and being forced into a reduced standard of living. Another way of stating risk is that it is the possibility that an investor's forecast of returns for the portfolio during his investment horizon is too optimistic. Unlike under CAPM, the real risk to an investor cannot be measured. In markets, there always are surprising and anomalous events. The investor must prepare for these events with risk management, which is discussed in more detail in Chapter 6. Risk management with the valuation cycle in mind reduces risk more than attempts to identify a risk that can be quantified and measured.

In addition to long-term valuation cycles, there are also shorter valuation cycles. A rational investor can try to identify the assets that are in long-term bull market valuation cycles and ride out any short-term cycles in those assets. Or the investor can try to identify the shorter-term cycles (of from one to five years) in assets and capture the profit opportunities within those cycles.

The consensus of investors at the extremes of the valuation cycle usually is wrong. Investors as a group are most bullish near a market top and are most bearish near a market bottom. The price of an investment cannot be pushed to an extreme without most investors having the same forecast and holding it with high intensity. While it is comforting to invest in line with the way most people are thinking, it is not likely to be profitable at the valuation extremes.

Investing with the majority view, however, can be profitable when valuations are not at an extreme. The valuation cycle is caused by the vast majority of investors moving from one extreme toward the other. That process can take years, and the shift pushes the markets in one general direction for some time. The persistence of beliefs is why many "contrarian" investment indicators often give false buy or sell signals. The signals generally work only at the extreme valuations. Most of the time, the majority of investors are right.

The wisdom of collective intelligence recently has received more positive attention and detailed study recently than in the past. The prime example of collective wisdom is the Internet search service, Google. It counts the links to each web page from other web pages and ranks them accordingly. In effect, Google has web page producers voting on the most valuable pages on each topic.

Crowds, especially markets, can be subject to periods when their decisions are less than intelligent. James Surowiecki, author of *The Wisdom of Crowds* (New York: Random House, 2004), argues that for the crowd to be wise, individuals must make decisions on their own while drawing on diverse sources of information. During the extremes of optimism and pessimism in the markets, people tend to act in response to others' actions rather than by making independent, rational decisions. To avoid the worst effects of these extreme periods, investors must apply Rational Beliefs Theory and try to determine if a market is reaching an extreme level of optimism or pessimism. The price of an asset can move in a different direction from the economic fundamentals. Asset prices also can move by a much higher percentage than the economic fundamentals. While studying the fundamentals of an investment is an important part of an investment process, the investor should be aware that market prices can stray from the fundamentals by significant amounts and for extended periods.

In the next chapters, we first see Rational Beliefs Theory applied to recent market history. This should demonstrate the validity of the key elements of the theory. Then we explore how Rational Beliefs Theory and market history can be used to develop an investment strategy and a portfolio that increase the likelihood of achieving the investor's goals.

# CHAPTER 5

# THE VALUATION CYCLE IN ACTION

E ach investment asset has a valuation cycle. The length of the cycle and the difference between the high and low points are not the same for all assets. But the cycle occurs for all assets in which investors can take profit-seeking positions, and it follows the process outlined by Rational Beliefs Theory.

The most-studied investments in the world are U.S. stocks and, in particular, the major stock market indexes. These indexes are the obvious choice for a practical application of Rational Beliefs Theory. They have a long history, accessible data, liquidity, and an established structure.

In this chapter we examine the behavior of U.S. stock indexes in the post-1981 period and compare it with the behavior anticipated by the theory. A brief review of the pre-1982 period is necessary to set the stage.

## STOCKS FOR THE LONG RUN?

In the 1970s and early 1980s few investors were interested in the U.S. stock market because of their dismal recent returns. The Dow Jones Industrial Average closed above 1,000 in 1966 and saw that level once or twice again in the ensuing years. Yet it was not able to remain above 1,000 for long and spent much of the post-1966 period below that level, often well below 1,000. Because the Dow Jones Industrial Average ("the Dow") is a price index and does not include reinvestment of dividends, investors in the index would have earned a higher return than is indicated by a simple tracking of the index values. The return still would be poor especially after adjusting for the high inflation of the period.

The Vietnam War, rising inflation, oil price shocks, political scandals, expanding government spending, and domestic civil disturbances all harmed the economy and markets, chasing investors from stocks. Investors were more attracted to hard assets—gold, silver, foreign currencies, and real estate—that provided an inflation hedge. The price/earnings ratios on the major stock market indexes sank to single digits, with the Dow's P/E (price/earnings) ratio bottoming at 7. By any measure, U.S. stocks were historically cheap, but few investors wanted to buy them.

As 1982 unfolded, the environment could not have been worse for stocks. Interest rates were sky high. An investor could earn about 18 percent annually by parking cash in a money market fund or certificate of deposit. The economy was nearing what turned out to the tail-end of a deep, long recession. (Officially, it was designated as two recessions with a brief recovery sandwiched between them.) Inflation consistently had been above 5 percent annually and was the major worry of consumers and investors. Few businesses undertook significant long-term planning or investments, because of the effects of high inflation and interest rates. The highest individual tax rate was 70 percent. Mexico sparked a banking crisis that threatened to bring down the world's financial system.

There were a lot of reasons not to invest in stocks and bonds. The cover story of *Business Week* for its August 13, 1979, issue was indicative—"The Death of Equities." The S&P 500 was at 105. The only stocks that interested most investors were those of oil and gold companies. (After the index rose 60 percent, *Business Week* had a different prognosis in its May 9, 1983, number. This time the cover story announced "The Rebirth of Equities.")

As we now know, this was perhaps the best time ever to invest in stocks and bonds and to sell hard assets. Powerful trends were beginning that would improve the economy and make financial assets much more profitable investments than they had been in the recent past. Yet

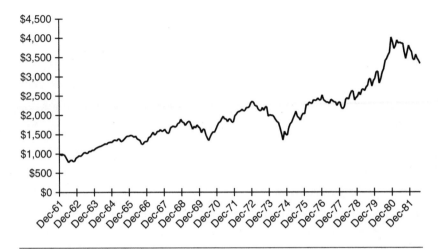

**FIGURE 5.1**    S&P 500: Value of $1,000 Invested on December 12, 1961

few investors saw the beginning of any of these trends and the favorable effect they would have on equities. The long bear market had sapped most of the hope investors had for future stock profits, and they did not believe any government policies would improve economic growth, reduce inflation, or boost stock prices. Several best-selling economic books at the time pushed the view that the economy was permanently small and perhaps shrinking. The books argued that policy makers should figure out ways to divide that smaller pie and give up trying to make it grow. In Rational Beliefs terminology, there was both a correlation of beliefs and persistence of beliefs about U.S. stocks among the vast majority of investors, and those beliefs were negative. The markets had reached a point of extreme pessimism as shown in Figure 5.1.

## THREE PROFITABLE SURPRISES

Investor attitudes and perceptions do not simply change. Events must occur to cause people to change their perceptions of the profitability of investments and convince them that structural changes were occurring in the economy or markets. In Rational Beliefs terms, the correlation of beliefs must change. The mass of investors gradually must move from being mostly pessimists, to a mixture of optimists and pessimists, to mostly optimists. This occurs when the investment models used by investors recommend changes in their portfolios.

This shift began in 1982 as investors became convinced that structural changes were occurring in the economy and markets that were positive for financial assets. The great bull market in stocks and bonds was triggered by at least three trends that made financial assets more profitable and changed investor perceptions of the future.

## The Great Disinflation

Inflation began rising in the early 1960s and rose steadily for two decades. By the early 1980s, most Americans believed inflation was an embedded and permanent feature of the economy. Then came Paul Volcker's appointment to chairman of the Federal Reserve Board in 1978. He began aggressive actions to reduce inflation and inflation expectations. These actions initially caused the severe downturns in the economy from 1980 to 1982, which increased investor pessimism.

Few factors are more important to investors than inflation. High and rising inflation erodes corporate profits and makes business planning difficult if not impossible. The result of high inflation is lower corporate profit growth. High inflation also eats away the value of both income and capital. Investors demand higher interest rates on bonds and very high potential returns from stocks before they will invest in these assets during inflationary times. Inflation contributed greatly to the poor returns stock and bond investors earned in the late 1960s and through most of the 1970s.

Fed Chairman Volcker and other central bankers around the world realized the danger of inflation and became committed to reducing it. Proof of their commitment is that the average rate of inflation declined in every five-year period from 1982 through 2000. Lower inflation led to lower inflation expectations. Lower inflation expectations help reduce interest rates as the charts show in Figures 5.2 and 5.3, make businesses more willing to invest, and make investors more willing to invest in stocks and bonds.

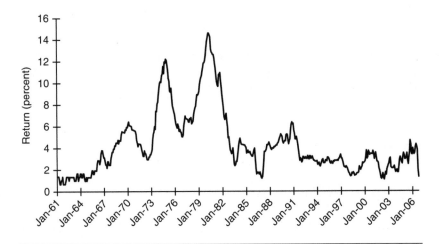

**FIGURE 5.2**   Consumer Price Index: January 1961 to January 2006

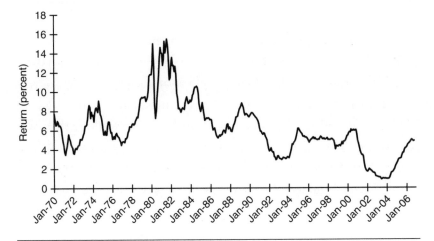

**FIGURE 5.3**   Six-Month Treasury Bill: January 1970 to January 2006

Investors at first did not realize that central bankers were serious about reducing inflation. When the Fed first reduced interest rates in August 1982 and sparked a stock market rally, there were few believers that this was the beginning of a long-term boom. Few believed that the corner had been turned on inflation and that interest rates were at the beginning of a long-term trend that would end with the lowest rates since World War II.

Over time, however, investors came to believe that the world's central bankers had resolved to keep inflation low. Views changed so much that by the early 2000s, investors believed deflation was more likely to be a problem than inflation. Federal Reserve Board Chairman Alan Greenspan even spoke of being concerned about deflation for the first time in 2003.

## Technology Triumphs

For much of the 20th century, the expectation was that technology would become the great savior of the economy. There were frequent forecasts that computers, robotics, and other inventions would make factory and office workers more productive. Fewer people would produce more goods at lower cost. This would reduce inflation, increase living standards, and make companies more profitable.

Beginning in the 1980s, after many false starts and disappointments, technology finally began to deliver on the expectations. Companies and individual workers became more productive and efficient. More goods and services were provided by fewer workers than was possible in the past, and the cost of technology kept decreasing. The United States was a particularly strong creator and beneficiary of this trend. Most of the technology developments of the 1980s and especially the 1990s came from the United States. The United States, because of its flexible market economy, adopted these technologies more quickly and effectively than did most other countries.

## Government Policies and the Global Economy

Government policies had a role in both the bear market before 1982 and the subsequent boom. The elections of Margaret Thatcher in the United Kingdom and Ronald Reagan in the United States ushered in policies of lower taxes and reduced regulations. These policies helped increase productivity and made investments more profitable and attractive. They also increased incentives for business and investors to invest capital. Along with the decline in inflation, these policy changes increased economic growth and made the economies stronger.

Another aid to economic growth as the bull market built was the decline of communism. That event increased free markets and free trade across the globe. Freer trade has several effects. It provides more potential customers for products. Trade also makes companies more competitive and efficient, because they must compete with producers and sellers from all over the globe instead of within their countries. Trade also increases the wealth of poorer countries, and that increases the potential customers for the goods and services of companies from established countries.

The expansion of free trade forces countries to compete with each other for international businesses. Governments are pressured to reduce regulations and taxes and generally make their laws more hospitable to business. The result was a virtuous cycle of free markets and better economic policies.

## THE VALUATION KICKER

These powerful trends brought lower inflation and lower interest rates. Bond investors profited from declining interest rates. The trends also initiated higher corporate profits. In fact, corporate profits in the United States began an extended period in which they grew faster than their long-term average growth rate. Rising corporate profits coupled with declining inflation and interest rates made stocks more attractive, and investors began to push the stock indexes higher.

The bull market in stocks and bonds continued almost unabated from August 1982 through March 2000. There were short, sharp declines in 1987 and 1990, and less severe drawdowns in 1984, 1994, 1996, 1997, and 1998. In general, it was one long upward surge in stocks and bonds with few interruptions. (Some argue that the equity bull market began at the severe bear market bottom in 1974 and that it was the bond bull market that began in 1982.)

The shift in investor attitudes from extreme pessimism to optimism and toward extreme optimism was reflected in the valuations of stocks. Stocks began the bull market at dirt cheap valuations, as discussed above. The price-earnings ratios of the major stock indexes were around seven at their bear market lows. While the economy and corporate profits grew in the post-1982 period, stock prices, as shown in Figure 5.4, increased at a faster rate.

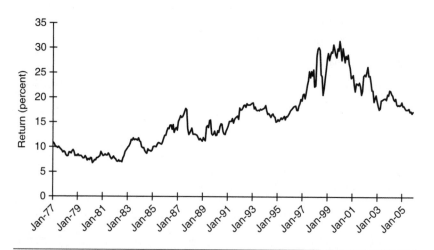

**FIGURE 5.4** S&P 500 Price/Earnings Ratio: January 1977 to January 2005

The P/E ratio, or multiple as many investors refer to it, is a reflection of investors' level of optimism or pessimism. The P/E ratio of a market index is an imperfect measure of market valuations and investor sentiments because the composition of the index has changed over the decades. The index once had a higher composition of cyclical manufacturing businesses and now has a greater percentage of less cyclical and higher growth service businesses. For these reasons, it should not be used by itself to make portfolio adjustments. Yet the measure is a useful proxy of the general trends in market valuations over time.

The multiple began this period at an extreme low, reflecting the predominance of pessimists among investors. It increased in a broken pattern throughout the bull market as the percentage of optimists among investors increased. One can see from a chart of the P/E ratio that it took many investors a while to shake off the pessimism of the 1970s and embrace the new economic environment. Even as the bull market progressed, there were times when investors became less optimistic and the P/E ratio declined. At times the decline in the multiple accompanied a decline in stock prices. At other times, the multiple declined because corporate profits surged faster than stock prices; investors apparently were not optimistic at times that the rate of profit growth would continue. These fluctuations reflected short-term changes in the ratio of optimists and pessimists among investors within a long-term trend during which the percentage of optimists was increasing.

We can see that the majority of investors began to throw off all doubts after 1994. That was a pivotal year in the bull market. Prior to that, from 1990 to 1991, the market experienced a recession and the first Gulf War. There also was a presidential election followed by a tax increase and forecasts of increased regulation. Those events increased pessimism at least for the short term, and the stock market indexes did not make much progress from 1990 through 1994.

The Federal Reserve made a series of unexpected interest rate increases in early 1994. This surprise caught a number of investors with too much risk or leverage in their portfolios. There were several widely reported financial disasters, perhaps the most significant involving Orange County, California, and Granite Capital, a hedge fund. Stocks fell sharply during the year but made a yearend recovery to be essentially flat for the year. The real action was in the bond market, which had one of its worst years on record.

By the end of the 1994, the Fed began to decrease interest rates. Also, a change in Congress helped inaugurate a fresh round of tax decreases along with some spending and regulatory restraint in the following years. A number of analysts also point to the initial public offering of Netscape during this period as a key source of optimism and the beginning of the technology boom in the economy and the stock market. Whatever the reasons, investors became progressively optimistic after 1994. There was a brief pause in the optimism in 1998 because of the Russian debt crisis and the failure of hedge fund Long-Term Capital Management discussed already in Chapter 1. Pessimists, however, retreated one by one after 1994.

While the expanding multiple puzzled many observers at the time, it is a normal part of the valuation cycle. As a stock bull market progresses, investors become more optimistic and become willing to pay more and more for each dollar of corporate profits. This willingness to pay more for corporate profits is what increases the valuation or multiple of stocks. As other investments trailed stock market returns through the late 1990s, more and more investors increased the allocation of stocks in their portfolios.

The rise in valuations accounts for much of the stock market gains after 1994. The major stock indexes increased more than 20 percent each year for five years, an unprecedented occurrence. This rate of return far exceeded the growth rates of the U.S. gross domestic product and corporate earnings.

As the stock boom and valuation expansion continued, many investors began to perceive the stock market as having little short-term risk and no long-term risk. They began to ignore valuations of stocks and were willing to pay ever higher prices for the stocks with the highest returns. Polls consistently showed that most investors believed it was reasonable to expect average annual returns of 15 percent or more.

The multiple surged rapidly in 1998 and 1999. This was the point of extreme optimism in the U.S. stock markets. A generation of investors now had traveled the full path from extreme pessimism to extreme optimism in stocks from 1982 through 2000. Investors loved stocks and believed they were the only investments worth owning. There now was a correlation of beliefs and persistence of beliefs among investors, and those beliefs were optimistic.

## MARKET DECOMPRESSION

It often is difficult to know, even in hindsight, which event or events cause the first group of investors to turn from optimism to pessimism and lead the market of investors on the trek from extreme optimism back to extreme pessimism. We do know that at some point in early 2000, investors became more skeptical about stock prices. The stock indexes peaked, and the valuations of the stock indexes began to decline. The case can be made that the shift actually began in 1998. From 1998 to 2000, only a small segment of the stocks that made up the major stock indexes appreciated. Other than large company growth stocks, stock prices were stagnant or declined during that period. The vast majority of stocks were in a bear market. The beginning of the bear market was disguised because the large company stocks were the only stocks that were appreciating, and because of the capitalization weighting of the major stock market indexes these large company stocks determine the returns of the indexes.

One trigger for the decline was that the Federal Reserve Board became concerned about both excessive stock prices and that rapid economic growth might increase inflation. To combat those forces, the Fed began tightening monetary policy and raising interest rates. Stock price valuations are affected by interest rates, at least over the long term. Rising rates make stocks less valuable and less attractive to investors. The Fed slowed the economy enough to cause a brief recession in 2001. The recession reduced corporate profits and the outlook for future profits, again making stocks less attractive to investors.

A temporary spurt in technology spending in the late 1990s is an often-overlooked factor in the last phase of the stock market rise and first phase of its decline.

In 1998 and 1999, corporations spent vast sums of money on new technology. The impetus for the spending was to avoid disasters that might spring from what was known as the Y2K computer bug. Briefly, the problem stemmed from the need to conserve hard disk space in the early days of computers. Thus, many older software programs recorded calendar years as two digits instead of four. Many computer analysts believed that havoc would be wreaked as the calendar moved from 1999 to 2000, causing computers to think it was 1900. There were forecasts of disasters ranging from computer crashes or freezes at small firms to shutdowns of major utility grids. To avoid any consequences, it was recommended that most software programs be rewritten or replaced. Several resourceful people made small fortunes warning about the Y2K problem and giving advice on how individuals and companies could protect themselves from the consequences of or even profit from the problem. Most companies decided that instead of revising existing programs they would do wholesale replacements and upgrades. This approach required purchases of new hardware, new software, and entire new systems. Technology spending soared.

What most people did not realize at the time was the extent to which the surge in technology spending was related to this one-time event. Companies would decrease technology spending dramatically after 1999. The pre-2000 technology spending would be a one-time surge, not a base on which future spending would build. As 2000 wore on, technology companies started to see revenues decrease instead of increase. Earnings forecasts were not met, and their stock prices started to decline.

Another problem, due to globalization of the economy, was a worldwide glut of production capacity in technology and some other industries. Corporate management and investors made mistakes estimating the worldwide supply and demand for many products. Since investors were richly rewarding growth (in many cases revenue growth even if a company wasn't profitable), corporate management generally did anything possible to expand capacity before 2000.

A contributor to the boom and bust was the enormous riches that befell many early venture capital investors as the bull market progressed. The spotlight that focused on these gains caused many others to try to get a slice of that pie. Record amounts of venture capital were thrown at businesses in the 1990s, and much of that money was not invested wisely. Since production was being expanded globally, it was difficult for management in one country to know all the new competing projects that were planned in other countries. When all that production came on line, the supply of various goods greatly exceeded demand.

## The Internet Bubble

Then came the so-called *Internet bubble.* The latest technology, the World Wide Web, was going to transform the way the world did business. Many Old Economy businesses would be replaced by New Economy businesses that sold goods and services over the Internet. Any company with a business plan and the right buzzwords could raise millions of dollars to start a web-based business. An adjunct of the Internet was telephony, telecommunications, and related technology. The popularity of the web would require new capacity in telephone lines, cable lines, wireless capacity, and related communications equipment.

While the Internet has changed business in many ways, it fulfilled only the more modest forecasts of its 1990s evangelists. The Internet has proved a valuable supplement to many Old Economy businesses, but it has replaced or revolutionized only a few. The Internet was so overpromoted and generated so much overinvestment that by 2000 there was a great deal of overcapacity in Internet-related technology.

Investors cannot be faulted completely for misunderstanding the growth in technology and the Internet. We know now that much of the hype surrounding the growth of the Internet stemmed from fraud at WorldCom. That firm was estimated to own about 50 percent of the "backbone" of the Internet, the hardware systems through which Internet communications pass. Unknown to most people, the folks at WorldCom were busy overstating the growth of the company's operations, including its Internet business. Projections on the growth of Internet traffic often were based on WorldCom's published results and its forecasts for the future. Since WorldCom's results were fraudulently overstated, investments others made were based on complete misconceptions about the growth of the Internet. As the fraud at WorldCom unraveled, investors began to realize that there might be problems with Internet-related investments because the growth of the Internet was exaggerated.

At first, the overall stock market did not suffer from these events. Internet, technology, and most growth company stocks fell sharply in 2000 and into 2001. Investors were slow to give up on their optimism, so the tech stocks had periodic rallies during the decline. In the meantime, many other stocks were appreciating. Recall that primarily large company growth stocks appreciated in 1998 and 1999, while the prices of other stocks fell or were unchanged. In 2000 and 2001, the stocks that lagged the previous two years appreciated. Once the technology miracle fizzled, many investors did not turn from the stock market. Instead, they bought stocks that did not participate in the last two years of the bull market and were selling at low valuations. Those stocks appreciated in 2000 and 2001, and their valuations increased. Because of the way the indexes are computed, the appreciation of these stocks did not provide much support for the returns of the indexes.

The terrorist attacks of September 11, 2001, caused a general decline in the economy and in all stock prices, but this also seemed short-lived. The markets bounced off their lows in late 2001 and into 2002. Many believed the bear market was over and easy stock market profits were back.

Subsequently, in mid-2002, the entire stock market began a sharp decline. Unlike in the recent past, there were no rolling bull and bear markets in sectors within the overall market. There was no shift from small company stocks back to the large company stocks. Even the value stocks that held up well through much of the bear market were dragged lower, as shown in Figure 5.5.

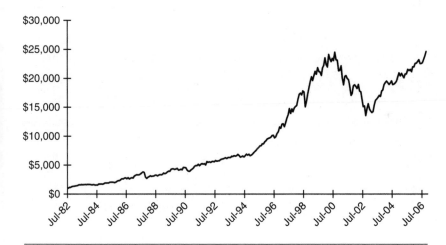

**FIGURE 5.5**  S&P 500: Value of $1,000 Invested on July 31, 1982

## THE CONSENSUS CHANGES

A series of events in 2002 finally converted many investors from optimists to pessimists.

The corporate accounting and fraud scandals, while involving a small number of companies, had a negative effect on investor confidence. The scandals taught investors that valuations and financial fundamentals matter. Investors became more skeptical of stories told by corporate management and by brokerage house analysts who might have conflicts of interest. They also realized that government regulators were not providing much protection for investors.

In addition, the Federal Reserve changed its policy. After September 11, 2001, the Fed flooded the economy with money to prevent the ensuing panic from turning into an economic collapse and deflation. Once the panic was over, the Fed withdrew that money, and the economy stagnated again.

Economies worldwide slowed. The glut of capacity became apparent, affecting many companies and economies. Many businesses were unable to raise prices and in fact saw prices steadily decrease. The notion that a deflation might be in the works became widespread.

The final straw probably was the realization that the consequences of terrorism would be around for some years. The buildup for the war with Iraq began. Terrorist organizations continued strikes around the globe. Governments and businesses incurred additional expenses to set up antiterrorist security, and there were many changes in the way people lived and did business.

The stock indexes hit a low in October 2002. Investors by all measures were pessimistic. This was in sharp contrast to the extreme optimism of only a few years before. Valuations on the stock market shrank considerably. The stock market indexes bounced off the October 2002 low for a few months, stalled again in early 2003, then surged starting March 2003. As of the end of 2006, stock market valuations of the major indexes after 2000 did not hit a low that would indicate extreme pessimism. Indeed, the P/E ratios of the S&P 500 and the Dow barely crossed as low as the long-term average. It was unclear whether the index lows of 2002 were secular bear market lows. It could be, as discussed earlier, that changes in the composition of the major indexes make historical P/E averages unreliable in determining when the markets reach a valuation low that indicates extreme pessimism. If so, then perhaps the October 2002 lows were the bottom of the bear market. Another possibility is that the 2000–2002 decline was only a cyclical decline in the secular post-1981 bull market that continues. Or it could be that the post-2002 rally was only a cyclical bull market within a longer secular bear market that began in 2000 and will continue for some years.

## INDIVIDUAL STOCKS AND THE VALUATION CYCLE

The valuation cycle applies to almost every investment asset. In this chapter we have applied it to stock market indexes. It also can be applied to individual stocks. A small group of large company growth stocks that were popular among investors in the late 1990s make for a good study.

In 1999 Dell Inc. had a P/E ratio of about 90. Hewlett-Packard's was at 45; Texas Instruments' was 116; and Wal-Mart Stores' was 56. These are extraordinarily high P/E ratios, well above long-term averages for these stocks and for the market indexes. After the stock market peak in early 2000, the earnings per share for these companies generally continued to increase. There were some pauses in the growth, especially from 2000 to 2002. But in general earnings per share rose after 1999.

By mid-2006, Dell had its earnings per share increase 110 percent, and Hewlett-Packard's rose 44 percent. For Texas Instruments the increase was 96 percent. Wal-Mart saw its earnings per share increase 135 percent. Yet, investors became much more pessimistic about these stocks than they were before 2000. By mid-2006, the price of Dell's stock had declined by about 60 percent from its peak, and it would decline further. Wal-Mart did the best of this group, losing only 31 percent of its value. Texas Instruments' stock declined 70 percent from its 2000 high, and HP declined 52 percent.

Clearly, as Rational Beliefs Theory explains and most investors know, stock prices over any period other than the very long term do not fluctuate with underlying economic fundamentals. Stock prices can rise faster than earnings as more investors become optimistic and persist in those beliefs. That is what happened to the prices of these stocks before 2000. Stock prices also can decline in the face of improving financial fundamentals if investors lose their optimism, as happened after 1999.

## FINDING A BOTTOM

It is not clear whether the market low in October 2002 was the low point for the post-2000 valuation cycle. The market indexes were at their low points for relatively brief periods. In addition, valuations as measured by P/E ratios of the indexes fell only to their long-term average level of around 15. They did not decline to a low that would indicate extreme pessimism based on the history of the measure, such as the multiple below 10 of the late 1970s and early 1980s. Table 5.1 shows the swing from extreme pessimism to extreme optimism and back toward pessimism using various measures of valuing the S&P 500. From the extremely low valuations in the early 1980s, the valuations increased in a stop-and-start

**TABLE 5.1** The Valuation Cycle in Action

|  | Jan. 1977 | Sept. 1981 | Sept. 1987 | Sept. 1995 | Dec. 1999 | Sept. 2002 | Dec. 2005 |
|---|---|---|---|---|---|---|---|
| Price/earnings ratio | 10.83 | 7.56 | 21.71 | 16.23 | 31.49 | 19.23 | 17.23 |
| Dividend yield | 4.70 | 6.25 | 2.77 | 2.40 | 1.27 | 2.14 | 1.99 |
| Price/book ratio | 1.41 | 1.09 | 2.25 | 2.83 | 5.42 | 2.51 | 2.85 |
| Price/sales ratio | 0.60 | 0.40 | 0.92 | 1.08 | 2.30 | 1.21 | 1.48 |
| Price/cash flow ratio | 5.73 | 4.06 | 8.28 | 9.18 | 19.11 | 11.17 | 11.53 |

manner until they hit the historic high valuations in late 1999 and early 2000. After the peak, valuations began to decline as investors became less optimistic.

It is worth noting the difference between the September 2002 and December 2005 valuations. The valuations actually are lower at the end of 2005 than they were in 2002. Yet stock prices increased significantly during that period and the economy also grew. Corporate earnings grew rapidly during the period, well above their historic average. Because investors were becoming less optimistic they were not willing to pay more for each dollar of corporate earnings. Stock prices improved far less than the underlying fundamentals of the companies in the index.

Some who study investment cycles point out that in a true bear market the levels of the major indexes retreat to at half or less of the bull market peak. Of the major U.S. stock indexes, only the NASDAQ declined that much. It retreated from a high of about 5000 to under 2000. The S&P 500 declined just over 45 percent, and the Dow Jones Industrial Index lost a bit over 30 percent.

As of late 2006 investors after 1999 did not reach the levels of extreme pessimism of the 1970s and early 1980s using measures such as the P/E ratio. Rational Beliefs Theory says that at some point investors will reach a level of extreme pessimism, but it does not say how long that will take or how the level can be measured. There also is no reason extremely low valuations must be reached before the percentage of optimists increases or even before another period of extreme optimism is reached. During the 1966–1982 period, the Dow Index reached 1,000 several times after 1966 before finally collapsing to the lows of 1972 and 1973. There were several times during the bull market before 2000 when it seemed the maximum point of optimism had been reached, and the markets seemed destined to head lower. But the markets recovered and investor optimism pushed markets to new highs. Each cycle is different. Mechanical rules cannot be used to determine when the tops and bottoms of a valuation cycle are reached.

The valuation cycle as explained by Rational Beliefs Theory applies to any investment asset, so this same analysis can be conducted for any other investment. The length of the cycles might not be as long for other investments as for U.S. stocks. The appreciation from top to bottom also might not be as high. But the basic cycle is the same and will be repeated over time.

In Chapter 6 we take the next step and learn how to use the knowledge of the valuation cycle and Rational Beliefs Theory to build and manage investment portfolios.

# CHAPTER 6

# FOXES AND
# REVEREND BAYES

## RATIONAL INVESTING IN
## IRRATIONAL MARKETS

Modern Portfolio Theory (MPT) taught investors to focus on risk as well as returns. Under MPT, the risk of either an individual investment or of a portfolio is its volatility. The risk of a portfolio is reduced by purchasing assets that have low correlations, or covariances, with each other, reducing the volatility of the portfolio. If the investor selects an efficient portfolio, it will have the highest return for that level of risk.

Rational Beliefs Theory builds on this advice. Investors learn from Rational Beliefs why volatility, correlations, returns, and expected returns change over time and why there is a valuation cycle. To reduce risk to the level the investor is willing to take and to increase the probability of reaching the goals, investors should not depend on long-term averages and relationships. Instead, investors need to be aware of the valuation cycle and where an asset is in the cycle.

Despite what some advocates of the Capital Asset Pricing Model (CAPM) say, forecasts of future market actions are an essential part of portfolio construction and were a key original element of MPT. Harry Markowitz in his early work on MPT said, "The process of selecting a portfolio may be divided into two stages. The first stage starts with observation and experience and ends with beliefs about the future performances of available securities." The efficient portfolio was not intended by Markowitz to be a buy-and-hold portfolio. The investor was supposed to recognize that investments fluctuate in price and that those fluctuations can cause returns to differ from the long-term average return for considerable periods.

The task for investors is to use the MPT process and Rational Beliefs Theory to develop a strategy for building portfolios that will achieve a desirable trade-off between risk and return.

## FOXES BECOME HEDGEHOGS

Many investors—after recognizing the valuation cycle in investments, the changing nature of correlations, and the shortcomings of using volatility as a measure of risk—realize that one way to avoid substantial losses and to meet investment goals is for the portfolio strategy to have flexibility. The portfolio allocation can change over time as Markowitz envisioned instead of being fixed.

The next step for these investors is to develop a strategy for changing portfolio allocations. It is at this point, unfortunately, that many foxes become hedgehogs, though perhaps a different breed of hedgehog. Realizing that portfolio allocations need to be changed periodically to maximize returns or reduce risk or both, many investors search for automatic systems to determine when to make those changes. Investors tend to believe that there are one or more signals or indicators that can be used to make portfolio changes. Many resources are spent sorting through data to locate these signals. Unfortunately, these resources largely are wasted if the goal is to find an infallible, automatic method for changing portfolio allocations.

Since the investment cycle is valuation related, it is logical to search for a valuation measure that indicates the tops and bottoms of the cycles. Much of the work done is on stocks and the stock market. Key valuation measures of the stock market are price-to-book value, dividend yield, price/earnings ratio, and the replacement value of corporate assets ($q$ ratio).

*Price-to-book value* (PBV) is the classic valuation measure. It was the preferred tool of the late investment legend Benjamin Graham, who wrote *The Intelligent Investor: A Book of Practical Counsel* (New York: Harper & Row, 1973) and coauthored the classic *Security Analysis* (New York: McGraw-Hill, 1934, 1940). Graham used this measure to determine which stocks to buy and sell. He also recommended using PBV to change the stock and bond allocations of a portfolio. When PBV indicated stocks were cheap, the percentage of stocks in the portfolio should be increased. When stocks were indicated as expensive, stocks should be no more than 50 percent of the portfolio.

PBV worked well for Graham, who invested primarily from the 1940s through the 1960s. As a reliable valuation measure, however, PBV ceased being effective around 1960. A likely reason for the change is inflation. Book value is the historic cost of corporate assets. Because of inflation, the original cost of long-term assets is not very meaningful. It is not reflective of the current value or what it would cost to replace the assets. In addition, as the economy shifted from manufacturing-based to service- and technology-based, physical assets became less important to companies and less important in determining their values. Whatever the reason, investors who hoped to duplicate Graham's success using PBV have been disappointed.

The *dividend yield* of individual stocks and of the stock indexes also is used by some as a key tool for building portfolios. The strategy, based on market history, is that the percentage of stocks in a portfolio should be reduced when the dividend yield on the major market indexes falls below three percent. Stocks should be increased when the dividend yield exceeds 6 percent as shown in Figure 6.1.

For many years the dividend yield was a very effective indicator, and many portfolios were managed successfully using the indicator. Yet the dividend yield for the S&P 500 Index consistently fell below 3 percent in 1992 and since then has remained below 3 percent. It was below 2 percent for much of the time after 1996. Investors who continued to use the dividend indicator to determine the allocation of their portfolios missed most of the great bull market of the 1990s.

As with PBV, circumstances and market structure changed. After the Great Depression and accompanying stock market crash, companies had to offer dividend yields that exceeded bond yields to attract

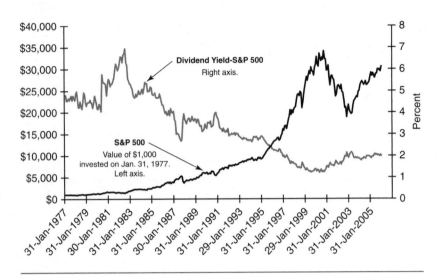

**FIGURE 6.1** S&P 500 Dividend Yield and Value of $1,000 Invested on January 31, 1977

investors. Stocks were considered primarily an income investment because of their high yields. After World War II, as the economy settled into an extended period of economic growth and stocks enjoyed a long bull market, stocks gradually came to be considered less risky. Investors were more willing to purchase them for capital gains as well as income. During the great bull market that began in 1982, investors became more and more comfortable with stocks and purchased stocks primarily or solely for capital gains rather than income. The tax law and other factors also encouraged companies to purchase their own stock in the market instead of paying dividends. Over time, the importance of dividends declined for both companies and investors. Dividend payouts and dividend yields declined. As dividends became less meaningful to investors, the dividend yield became both less volatile and less useful for valuing a stock or the stock market.

*Price/earnings (P/E) ratios* are the most widely used measure of stock market valuations. Many investors believe that stocks are overvalued or at least highly valued when the P/E ratio exceeds 20. Stocks are relatively inexpensive when the P/E ratio is below 10 and are bargains when the ratio is around seven. The long-term average P/E ratio for the S&P 500 Index is around 15. A general rule many investors developed is to reduce stock holdings when the P/E ratio is above 20 and increase stocks in the portfolio when the P/E ratio is below 10.

Only half of this formula is supported by the data.

When the P/E ratio is low, increasing allocations to stocks proves highly profitable. For years, when the P/E ratio was below 10, the average return for the next year was 16.2 percent. For the next three years the average annual return was 14.8 percent. And for the next 5 and 10 years the average annual returns were 15.1 percent and 14.2 percent, respectively.

The P/E ratio, however, is not a good indicator of when to reduce stock holdings. Stocks have shown that they can continue to appreciate for years after the P/E ratio exceeds 20. For the next one, three, and five years after the P/E ratio exceeds 20, the S&P 500 generates returns exceeding its long-term average. On average, it is only over the next 10 years after the P/E ratio exceeds 20 that the index generates annualized returns below the long-term average. The P/E ratio is another mechanical rule that is not reliable on its own for portfolio management.

It also is likely that structural changes make the history of the P/E ratio unreliable in evaluating the meaning of the current level. Manufacturing and other cyclical businesses used to be more significant factors in the economy and the market indexes than they are today. Now, service industries are far more important. These businesses are less volatile than manufacturing businesses and not prone to the extreme cyclical highs and lows of manufacturing. Service industries tend not to hit the cyclical valuation lows of manufacturing. Because of those changes, extreme pessimism might be indicated by P/E levels above the cyclical lows of the past.

The $q$ ratio was developed by academic economists as a measure of the stock market. It attempts to measure stock prices as a percentage of the replacement value of corporate assets. It updates Ben Graham's PBV by accounting for the effects of inflation, technology, and other factors. Yet the measure has not proven useful to investors as a portfolio management tool.

Investors also seek indicators outside the stock market as guides for making portfolio changes. In the belief that trends in the broad economy presage stock market activity, there are many rules of thumb often repeated among investors or in the financial media. Investors often develop these rules based on anecdotes, personal observations, or a selective review of history. This conventional wisdom is refuted by data and experience. Interest rates, bonds, and the economy are not reliable indicators of stock market returns over any short period. There are correlations between some of these data and the stock market over the very long term, but not during shorter periods. Investors who understand Rational Beliefs Theory should expect this lack of connection, and we saw examples of it in the previous chapter. The theory explains why stock prices can change without a related change in underlying fundamentals or by a greater degree than the fundamentals.

Another group of tools used by some investors to make portfolio management decisions is technical analysis. The tools used vary considerably. Some investors examine price charts of individual stocks or the market indexes. Others examine particular statistics, such as trading volume, the number of stocks increasing in price compared to those decreasing in price, and more complicated measures. There are quite a few tools that can be classified as part of technical analysis.

Research does not support the notion that one or a small number of technical analysis tools effectively forecast investment changes. Even advocates of technical analysis use multiple data points to make decisions and speak in terms of probabilities rather than certainties. The strongest case that can be made for technical analysis is that the tools identify the establishment and strength of trends and can indicate when a trend might be nearing an end. The tools of technical analysis, however, do not forecast either long-term or short-term turning points in investments.

## WHY INDICATORS FAIL

A piece of data becomes a portfolio management tool after research—or experience—shows it to work over some period of time. Experience reveals that none of these tools remains consistently reliable. The search for certainty in portfolio management fails because of the nature of the investment markets.

Consider the 39-week moving average, which once was very profitable as a tool for changing portfolio allocations. It is simple and easy to follow. More importantly, the tool would have investors owning primarily stocks during rising markets and out of stocks during the major portion of declines. Yet, the 39-week moving average has not produced profitable results in years.

The strategy is simple: Sell stocks when the closing value of a market index is below its moving average for the last 39 weeks. Buy stocks when the index value is above the average. The system was derived through back testing, or data mining. It worked for a while in practice; but over time the technique ceased being effective. The tool stopped delivering its key value: a sell signal that avoids big losses in major market declines.

This life cycle of the 39-week moving average indicator is similar to that of other automatic investing tools—both those discussed previously and many others not discussed here. Before seeking or adopting such automatic investment indicators as part of their strategies, investors should consider the research on markets and investment signals. A review of that research reveals several reasons why the search for automatic portfolio management tools is futile.

• *Markets are dynamic.* Relationships that seemed fixed in the past are likely to change in the future. Economist Andrew Lo refers to this as the *Adaptive Markets Hypothesis.* He likens the process to Darwin's Theory of Evolution in nature. The markets and the economic environment continually change, and investors must adapt to the changes. Lo also believes that emotions play a part in market evolution and change. The result is that at times prices cannot be trusted; they stray from underlying fundamentals. This hypothesis is consistent with but not as fully developed as Rational Beliefs Theory.

• *Turning points are easy to identify only in hindsight.* It is easy to look back at a chart of P/E ratios and identify the high points of the market. It is more difficult to determine what will be the high or low point for the current market cycle. In the bull market that ended in 2000, many investors sold their stocks early. As the P/E ratio climbed through 20 to 25, 30, and eventually over 40, a group of investors concluded that each new level had to be the high-water mark for the cycle. Yet, the stock indexes continued rising beyond the point many investors thought would be possible. The same process is likely to occur with any statistic or indicator.

• *Once they are well known, market indicators stop working.* Economists debate exactly why this occurs, but it is clear that once a critical mass of investors is exposed to the same "success secret," it stops being successful. The classic example is the January Effect, which we discussed earlier in this book. In the 1960s, academic researchers exposed the tendency in the United States for stocks to decline late in the year and rise the following January. Investors could profit by selling stocks in November, purchasing them on the last trading day of December or first trading day of January, and holding them until the end of January. Additional research determined that the strongest gains from the January Effect were reaped by small company stocks and in the first half of January.

The *January Effect* became widely discussed among academics and eventually among investment professionals, the financial media, and individual investors. At least one book was devoted entirely to the topic. After all the publicity, the January Effect ceased to reoccur consistently. As more and more investors learned about and anticipated it, market behavior changed and the anomaly disappeared.

• *Most conventional wisdom is not well researched.* It is not unusual for an investment rule or pattern to be stated in the financial media or be widely accepted among investment professionals. It also is not unusual for those beliefs to exist without the support of rigorous research. Investors should not use such wisdom to manage their portfolios unless they have reviewed the research and seen for themselves that the pattern is reliable. Even the bits of conventional wisdom that are supported by research usually show only a tendency for markets to behave in a certain way. The cause-and-effect relationship in the rules does not occur 100 percent of the time. If it occurs more than 50 percent of the time, that is enough for many people to consider it a rule. However, when a relationship holds up less than 100 percent of the time, the investor is risking capital by following the rule and assuming the relationship will hold. The losses from the minority of instances when the rule does not work can offset the gains from when it does work.

• *Markets are complicated.* Prices of investments are influenced by multiple factors. Even when a relationship is discovered between investment prices and a factor, the investor should determine the reason for the relationship. It could very well be a coincidence that a relationship shows up in the data. If so, at some point the apparent relationship will break down, to the investor's detriment.

• *The beginning and ending points for the data affect the results.* Some researchers limit their inquiries to certain time periods because of either a lack of resources or a specific interest in the time period. Broader research, however, often shows that the results change if the time period tested changes.

For example, a study—"The Halloween Indicator: Sell in May and Go Away" (*American Economic Review*, December 2002)— investigated the *Halloween Indicator*, the notion that most positive stock market returns are clustered between mid-October and May 1. This theory backs the popular trading rule: Sell in May and go away. The study found that since 1970 in 38 of 39 stock markets worldwide the rule held. An investor can increase returns by owning stocks only during the October-through-May period. Yet the study was limited to the period from 1970 onward because of a lack of quality data for most markets. The *Wall Street Journal* ("Be Careful of Buying This Line: Halloween's a Good Time to Buy," 7 October 2006) echoed a study in the *Hulbert Financial Digest*, which used Dow Jones Industrial Average data for a much longer period and found that, for the years before 1970, the returns were about equal for the October through May period and for the rest of the year. The rule was not validated by the longer-term study.

This often is the case with historic studies. Changing the time period studied changes the results.

• *Anomalous periods can influence long-term results.* Before using the results of a long-term study, investors should examine the results in shorter periods. They might find that the long-term average results were heavily influenced by excessive gains or losses in one period. Repeating the long-term results depends on that period's results being repeated.

Professors Grant McQueen and Steven Thorley took a look at a strategy called the *Foolish Four*, described in *The Motley Fool Investment Guide: How the Fools Beat Wall Street's Wise Men and How You Can Too* (New York: Simon & Schuster, 1996). The strategy as described in the book outperformed the Dow from 1973 to 1993. To further test the theory, the professors looked at additional data from 1952 to 1972. During this period they found that the Dow beat a portfolio using the Foolish Four strategy. They also tested the strategies for the six years following 1993 and were unable to establish the strategy's superiority. Perhaps the strategy was a winner only during the 1973 to 1993 period.

Hedgehogs frequently are searching for formulas, signals, and automatic trading strategies such as those described so far in this chapter. This "data mining" process is simply searching through market and economic data for successful investment approaches. The search might be for correlations, patterns, or trading rules. Data mining has become more widespread with the price decline in powerful computers and the increased availability of affordable databases.

Data mining results must be used with great caution. They are subject to misinterpretation and overstatement. A classic study done to warn against data mining is David Leinweber's *Stupid Data Mining Tricks: Over-Fitting the S&P 500* (New York: First Quadrant Monograph, 1997). Leinweber used a CD-ROM from the United Nations that contained a great deal of economic data from most countries around the globe. He sought the data that was best correlated with the performance of the S&P 500 Index. The study's conclusion was that the key economic data, tied to the S&P 500 75 percent of the time, was butter production in Bangladesh!

## CHAOS, COMPLEXITY, AND CRITICAL STATES

Disciplines outside of economics and finance also help explain why hedgehog approaches do not work and why investors should not seek automatic indicators or fixed strategies to guide their investment decisions. These disciplines include *chaos theory* and *complexity theory*. Normally the domain of physicists and other scientists, the disciplines are the study of systems, specifically the study of how individual actors in a system organize and integrate into the larger system, and how their actions affect the system. The researchers believe that their work can explain how all systems operate, including economies and markets.

One key insight from the work is that the individuals in the markets learn, grow and adapt, and they do so quickly. As a result, the market or system also is adapting. An investment market is a growing, changing network. It is not a fixed organization in which the same actions will result in the same effects. A market evolves and adapts, because the individuals that make up the market evolve and adapt.

Another key insight from other fields that can benefit investors is the point known as the *critical state*. Researchers have studied earthquakes, market crashes, ecological disasters, epidemics, traffic jams, and information flow in business organizations. The goals of the studies included learning how stable situations turned into disasters, how to predict a disaster, and how to forecast the size of a disaster. What the research is showing is that many of these cannot be predicted.

Systems tend to build themselves to a critical state. This is the point at which the system is highly susceptible to change. For example, the next grain of sand dropped onto a sand pile could trigger a collapse or an avalanche. Or the critical state can be the point at which adding one more degree of heat to water could make it boil, or subtracting one more degree turns it to ice. The critical state is the point at which some action could trigger a change in the basic nature or character of the system. An imperfect analogy might be the "tipping point."

A concept—developed in concert with the critical state—is that as a system builds toward the critical state it develops "fingers of instability" that run throughout the system. They are of different sizes, and each finger has the potential for being part of a different size reaction. Consider a sand pile, an example in *Ubiquity: Why Catastrophes Happen* by Mark Buchanan (New York: Three Rivers Press, 2001). After the sand pile has grown and evolved to the critical state, there are different fingers of instability throughout the pile. Drop a grain of sand on one of the fingers, and a minor avalanche is triggered. But drop the additional grain of sand on one of the larger fingers of instability, and the entire pile could collapse.

Every avalanche begins with one grain of sand too many being dropped on the pile. The size of the avalanche has nothing to do with the size of the additional grain, or with any special situation regarding the sand pile when compared to another sand pile. Instead, the size of the avalanche has to do with the critical state and the fingers of instability, which makes it possible for an avalanche of any size to be triggered.

Another interesting insight from this field is that stability leads to instability. A different way of saying this is that the longer the period of stability before a catastrophe, the more likely it is that the unstable event will be severe. The theory is that the more comfortable the actors in a system are with the current conditions, the more likely it is that the conditions will persist. The continuation produces more and greater fingers of instability, and those fingers are more likely to be connected to each other. This process increases the potential for a severe catastrophe.

This insight is easy to apply to investment markets. As the stock market rises without an extended correction, investors become more comfortable with stocks and expect higher returns with low risk. They take more risk in their portfolios. Over time, more and more investors have riskier portfolios. The prices of riskier assets increase because of the additional buyers. Other actors in the economy also are likely to be taking riskier actions such as adding debt or riskier debt or buying exotic financial instruments. These actions all increase the probability that when the critical state is reached and the period of instability arrives, it is likely to be longer and more serious than if it had occurred earlier in the process.

This process also explains what the investment world calls "fat tails," which were discussed in Chapter 1.

The probability of events in most activities can be grouped into what statisticians call the bell curve or a normal distribution. The bulk of events occur in the middle of the curve, and only a few events occur on the sides, or tails, which gradually taper down to zero. The small or narrow tails of the bell curve mean that extreme events have a very low probability of occurring. But studies of investment history show that the probability distributions of markets have fat tails. The extreme events occur with some regularity and have a higher probability of occurring than would be the case under a normal distribution.

It appears that actors in the investment markets delay the period of instability until many fingers of instability have been created. That increases the likelihood that when the critical state is reached, the period of instability will be more serious than it might have been. The extended periods of stability lead to greater instability.

Complexity theory also supports an element of Rational Beliefs Theory. From complexity theory we have the concept of a positive feedback loop. This occurs when actors take an action primarily because most other actors are doing the same. We see something akin to positive feedback loops in the extreme phases of bull and bear markets. As a bull market approaches a peak, investors buy regardless of the fundamentals or price. They buy because other investors are buying and returns are increasing. In the worst stage of a bear market, investors sell primarily because other investors are selling and returns are declining. This process is described by the persistence of beliefs and correlation of beliefs of Rational Beliefs Theory.

Complexity and chaos theory teach us that systems grow, change, and adapt. Systems also veer from stability to instability, and the trigger point or event that causes a change is unpredictable. Investment markets are systems that have all these characteristics. Investors should realize that they will not be able to derive a single formula or algorithm that will spot changes and always be valid. Investors need to adjust their strategies continually. In other words, long-term investment success is unlikely to fall to those who adopt the hedgehog approach of learning one or two big things and using those ideas to develop portfolio strategies that are never modified.

## ENTER REVEREND BAYES

A foxlike investor knows that the portfolio should be adjusted over time because of the valuation cycle described in Rational Beliefs Theory. Without making propitious adjustments, the investor could suffer an extended period of below-average returns and fail to achieve his or her goals. Because markets change and adapt over time, the foxlike investor should not use mechanical formulas or automatic signals to make the portfolio adjustments. A method that seemed to work in the past will stop being an effective indicator of market changes at some point. How, then, should investors manage their portfolios to avoid long periods of below average returns?

Investors should consider the work of the Reverend Thomas Bayes.

Bayes's name is familiar to many investors and investment professionals, but primarily for the statistical techniques to which his name is attached. They know little else about him or how his thinking can help develop effective portfolio strategies.

Yet some successful people in the economic and financial worlds know and admire Bayes for more than a statistical formula. One such person is Alan Greenspan, former chairman of the Federal Reserve Board. Despite apparent success in steering monetary policy while chairing the Fed, Greenspan was criticized by some economists and investment professionals for not belonging to a particular economic school of thought or clearly articulating a monetary policy philosophy. Outsiders often were unable to anticipate Fed actions under Greenspan or explain why actions were taken. As Greenspan was leaving his tenure at the Fed, the *Wall Street Journal* published a profile about him (Greg Ip, "Greenspan's Legacy Rests on Results, Not Theories," 31 January 2006) explaining this situation. Greenspan had "portrayed himself as a 'Bayesian." (Not a lot is known about Thomas Bayes today. He was born in London in 1702. Because of his religion, Oxford and Cambridge were closed to him so he enrolled at the University of Edinburgh to study logic and theology. Though Bayes's primary vocation was a Presbyterian minister, he was also a mathematician and published two books during his lifetime: a work of theology and a defense of Isaac Newton's calculus against the attacks of Bishop George Berkeley. This latter book combined both theology and mathematics.)

Bayes died in 1761 and it is a book that was published posthumously on which his reputation rests, *Essay Towards Solving a Problem in the Doctrine of Chances* (1764). It contains *Bayes's Theorem of Estimation,* which is taught in all basic statistics and probability courses and known simply as *Bayes's Estimation* or *Bayes's Theorem.*

Bayes's Theorem is now what we call *statistical inference.* He addressed problems in which future results need to be estimated because past data is known, but not all current data is known. In the classic Bayes problem, past data about the population being studied are known. To estimate the future results, the past data are combined with a sample of current data. The main innovation from Bayes is that, instead of making a specific estimate, a range of possible results known as a probability distribution is calculated. The answer might be along the following lines: There is a 20 percent probability the stock market index will rise 8 percent or more in the next 12 months; a 30 percent probability it will rise between zero percent to 7.9 percent, a 30 percent probability it will decline up to 7.9 percent, and a 20 percent probability is will decline 8 percent or more. Under the Bayes approach, the answer does not have to be constant or a single number. Instead, the answer can be variable and can be expressed as a probability distribution. Another Bayes innovation is that the past data used to estimate the future can be objective or it can be opinion or estimates if objective data is not available.

We do not need to delve in any more detail regarding Bayes, his theorem, and the criticisms of it. This summary is sufficient to show us what is valuable for investment decision making.

## Investing as Risk Management

Too often investors manage their portfolios by trying to determine the most likely course of the markets over a given future period. After arriving at a forecast, they adjust their portfolios to maximize profits under the forecast scenario. We know, however, that it is very difficult to develop an accurate forecast of the markets. If one accurate forecast is very difficult, developing a series of accurate forecasts over time is unlikely to happen. When a portfolio is allocated to maximize profit from particular forecasts, then at regular intervals it is likely to lose a significant portion of its value when forecasts are not accurate.

The Bayes approach often is referred to today as *risk management.* It is a good tool for investors to use, and it can be used without having to learn to perform Bayesian statistical calculations.

What Bayes meant is that decision makers should not try to determine the most likely outcome and act under the assumption of that outcome. Instead, the decision maker should determine the range of possible outcomes and base actions on the results that would be occurred within that likely range.

Let us first consider how a non-Bayesian might manage a portfolio. The investor would make a stock market forecast for the year. If he (or she) forecasts that the stock market would rise more than 8 percent, he likely would allocate 100 percent of the portfolio to stocks. If he determined that the stock index would decline more than 8 percent, it is likely that he would sell all stocks and buy bonds or some other investment. For forecasts that the stock index returns would be somewhere between an 8 percent loss and an 8 percent gain, the portfolio probably would be allocated to a combination of stocks and bonds and perhaps other assets.

If the forecast is wrong, the investor is holding the wrong portfolio. More importantly, the investor risks incurring large losses if the forecast is very different from actual results. If the investor forecasts an 8 percent gain but the market declines more than 8 percent, the portfolio loses substantial value. Likewise, if the investor forecasts a greater than 8 percent loss but stocks rise more than 8 percent, the opportunity to earn substantial gains is lost.

The non-Bayesian investor, instead of making forecasts, might try to use one or more of the automatic signals as discussed earlier in this chapter. Changes would be made according to the signals. This would be very similar to investing based on a forecast. Each change in the signal would be the same as a change in the forecast, and the portfolio would be adjusted to maximize gains based on that signal or forecast.

The risk of incurring a large loss or missing all of a potential unexpected gain is reduced by using probability distributions and risk management. Instead of adjusting the portfolio to succeed if one forecast is correct, the investor estimates a range of probable market results for the year. The portfolio is invested so that it will earn a reasonable return should the actual results be within the range of probable results. The portfolio would have some diversification. It would hold different assets so that one or more holdings will appreciate under each likely scenario. In addition, assets that would decline in the likely scenarios but appreciate only in unlikely scenarios would have little or no weight in the portfolio.

This means if the stock market has a very good year, the highest potential returns will not be earned, and modest losses might be incurred if actual results are very different from what was considered the most likely scenario. This approach also means the portfolio has a low chance of incurring a large loss from unexpected results and a high probability of earning a good return should actual market returns fall anywhere in a range of possible market outcomes.

Another element of a Bayesian approach is contingency plans. As the year develops, the case would evaporate for some scenarios that were considered possible at the start of the year. Other scenarios would seem to be more likely as events unfold and more information is known. The portfolio would be adjusted to adapt to the new information and changing circumstances. This would be a constant process for the Bayesian investor as new information is learned.

One can see the similarities between the Bayesian and the fox. The fox does not seize on one big idea and cling to it. Instead, the fox adjusts her (or his) thinking based on changed circumstances and new information. Similarly, the Bayesian examines past results and a sample of current information to construct a range of possible outcomes for the future. The Bayesian avoids the temptation to draw one conclusion from this data. Actions are based on the range of likely outcomes, not on one expected outcome. Both the fox and the Bayesian usually avoid making one strong, precise forecast and acting on it. They do so only if the examination of past data and a sample of current outcomes indicates a high probability of success.

The investor can use the Bayesian approach to risk management in either of two ways. One way is very scientific and methodical. The investor can use actual data to develop formulas that arrive at a precise probability distribution of possible investment outcomes. This is impractical for most investors and needlessly complicated. In addition, we know from information presented earlier in this book that markets change. A forecast of that type is likely to give a false confidence of accuracy, and reliance on past data will miss changes in the markets.

The other way is use the broader principles of both Bayes and Modern Portfolio Theory. Instead of focusing on returns, focus on risk management when building a portfolio. Determine the potential risks of each potential investment and of the portfolio as a whole. Then, the investor should ask: "Which risks am I willing to take, and which do I want to avoid?" The portfolio is adjusted to eliminate risks the investor does not want to take.

So far, this discussion has been philosophical and abstract. At this point we can get more specific about how the insights of Rational Beliefs Theory and Reverend Bayes can be used to develop strategies and portfolios. There are a number of ways these insights can aid investors. We will discuss several of them in the rest of this chapter. One important concept is that there is not one correct investment strategy or portfolio. There are a number of avenues available for the investor to achieve reasonable investment goals while taking a tolerable amount of risk. Another important concept is that investment success depends on moving beyond the simple purchase of stocks and bonds and holding a basic allocation of them in a fixed portfolio. The specific composition of a successful portfolio changes over time as circumstances and the markets change. An adaptable strategy or the use of more than one approach increases the probability that an investor can reach his or her goals.

## HEDGING ONE'S BETS

One way to manage risk and reduce exposure to the valuation cycle is to invest less in traditional "plain vanilla" investments and more in nontraditional investment vehicles such as those generically known as *hedge funds*.

There are believed to be over 9,000 hedge funds—but really no one knows. Many in the investment industry believe that the best talent is gravitating to hedge funds because higher incomes are possible. There was a substantial flow of money into hedge funds after the market peak in 2000, and the vehicles generated a lot of media attention. Yet, despite the increased attention, hedge funds are frequently misunderstood.

Traditionally, a hedge fund is an investment pool or partnership in which the manager "hedges" against a market decline by buying some stocks and selling others short. There are different ways to hedge now because of financial innovations, but the basic hedging strategy is to own assets that the manager likes and sell short assets the manager dislikes. Now, a hedge fund means something else. An investment fund is subject to a lower level of federal and state regulations if it restricts its investors to what the law defines as "qualified investors" and does not advertise to other investors. Qualified investors generally are wealthy individuals or institutions such as pension funds and endowments. These investors are believed either to be sophisticated or to have ready access to sophisticated advice, so they do not need the protection of mutual fund regulations. Today, "hedge fund" refers to any investment fund that avoids mutual fund regulations. As the *Wall Street Journal* refers to them, hedge funds are "lightly regulated investment vehicles."

Most hedge funds specialize in a particular investment niche, and there are many investment strategies in the hedge fund world. There is the traditional strategy described above, known as the long/short strategy and a variation of that known as market-neutral strategies. These involve buying and selling short different stocks so that the positions largely offset each other and the fund does not rise or fall with the market indexes. Other common strategies involve convertible bonds, merger arbitrage (buying and selling stocks involved in mergers or takeovers), distressed situations (bankrupt or near-bankrupt companies), and special situations. There also are macrostrategy funds that try to identify and take advantage of changes in major markets such as stock indexes, currencies, and commodities. A macrostrategy fund could be invested in almost any market over time. There also are hedge funds that specialize in particular markets or industries. A major segment of the hedge fund world is composed of multistrategy funds that have teams or subfunds pursuing all or most of the strategies already described.

A hedge fund might or might not use leverage, or debt, in its investment positions. Some funds invest in opportunities that have small profit opportunities. They increase investors' returns by using debt to invest in these opportunities and increase the returns on their investment capital. Other funds seek high returns and try to increase those returns by investing with debt or other leverage such as futures and options. Some hedge funds avoid all debt and leverage.

A unique feature of a hedge fund is its fees, which are much higher than traditional money management fees. A hedge fund first charges an annual management or administrative fee of 1 percent to

2 percent of the fund assets, though some charge even higher fees. In addition, the fund management is paid 20 percent of all investment profits, and some hedge funds take as much as 50 percent of profits. Most hedge funds have a "high-water mark." Suppose a hedge fund had $1 billion in assets and a 50 percent return one year. It now is a $1.5 billion fund. (We will ignore the effect of fees.) The second year it loses money. The managers will not earn a profit participation the second year. In addition, they will not earn a profit participation in subsequent years until the fund again reaches the $1.5 billion level (ignoring fees, new investments, and distributions for this example).

Investors are attracted to hedge funds for several reasons. One appealing feature of many hedge funds is low correlation with the stock market indexes. The volatility of a fund's value is not tied to the ups and downs of the equity market indexes. A hedge fund with low correlation to stocks can hold its value or produce high returns when stocks are in a bear market. In addition, an investor can construct a diversified portfolio of multiple hedge funds in which the funds are not correlated with each other. The hedge funds will have good and bad years at different times. That provides a much smoother return pattern than a traditional portfolio.

Hedge funds also seek what are called absolute returns instead of relative returns. A relative return is one measured by a market index. For example, an equity mutual fund is measured by its returns relative to a market index. If the stock index declines 20 percent, a mutual fund is considered good if it declines only 15 percent. An absolute return fund seeks to earn a positive return regardless of how the stock market index (or any other index) is performing. Some absolute return funds seek any positive return. Others seek to earn higher than the Treasury bill rate, the inflation rate, or those rates plus a set percentage. For example, a fund might state that its goal is to earn the 90-day Treasury bill rate plus 3 percent.

Absolute returns are particularly attractive to pension funds, since the required contribution rates from their employers rise or fall with investment returns. If investment returns are more predictable and are not tied to stock market fluctuations, cash management is easier for the employer because annual contributions are more level and predictable.

Many hedge funds also offer lower risk, as measured by volatility, than a portfolio that is mostly equity based. Not all hedge funds have this characteristic. Those that use a lot of leverage or seek high returns in volatile markets might be more risky and volatile. But one feature of many hedge funds is their ability to manage portfolios so that there are smaller annual fluctuations in value than in the stock market indexes.

## The Less Glamorous Side

Hedge funds are not without disadvantages, even to those who are able to meet the restrictive entrance requirements.

The funds have low liquidity, meaning that it is not easy to exit a fund. Most allow investors the return of all or part of their investments only during a specific time frame each year, and requests for funds must be received before the withdrawal period. A standard provision is that distributions will be made only at the end of October, and requests must be received in writing at least 60 days before the distribution date. In addition, an investor must leave an investment in the hedge fund for a minimum period before taking a distribution. The usual "lock-up period" is one year, but some funds have lockup periods of from two to five years.

The information flow from hedge funds is very different than that of funds subject to mutual fund regulations. Legally required disclosures are minimal, and many hedge funds do not fully disclose their investment strategies or their current or recent portfolio holdings. This is known in the business as a lack of transparency. The funds argue that the information is proprietary, and they cannot risk letting competitors learn their strategies and holdings. Some hedge funds reveal little more to investors than their returns. Others are more forthcoming about their strategies and recent positions. The lack of information can make it difficult for investors to evaluate funds before investing and deciding whether or not to continue holding a fund they own.

The surge in the popularity of hedge funds created new problems for investors. Most hedge fund strategies can be implemented successfully only with a limited amount of capital. Too much money invested in a particular strategy disrupts the market and takes away the profit opportunity. Accordingly, most of the best hedge funds are not accepting new investors and have not for years. Many close to new investors soon after inception. Investors often must choose from funds that do not have the best records and from new funds with untested managers.

This problem is significant because there is a wide performance gap between the best and worst hedge funds, whether compared annually or over longer periods. The difference is far greater than among mutual funds. The lack of transparency in many hedge funds and the restrictions funds have on new investors already make it difficult for an investor to select hedge funds. The wide dispersion of returns means that the investor faces a much higher selection risk with hedge funds. Selecting a fund that performs among the lowest quartile of funds with similar strategies earns the investor much lower returns than someone who invested in a top-performing or even an average hedge fund. An investor who cannot gain entry to the better hedge funds likely would be better off not investing in these funds.

The high number of hedge funds also means that there are quite a few funds using essentially the same strategies and trying to exploit the same opportunities. The large amount of capital pursuing the same investments or strategies can alter the markets and limits the profits available to these funds. This is similar to the effect, which we studied earlier, of an investment strategy or indicator losing its effectiveness once it is well known. A large amount of capital pursuing the same investment or strategy also can increase volatility of that investment or strategy.

For some investors, a difficulty is that hedge funds are an investment vehicle, not an asset class. As can be gleaned from the review of different hedge fund strategies, there is a great deal of diversity and variability among the strategies used by hedge funds. An investor might have difficulty deciding where a fund fits in a portfolio and which other investments best complement it. Some investors treat their hedge funds as a separate asset. Others try to match individual hedge funds to different asset classes. Before deciding to put capital into one or more hedge funds, an investor needs to determine why hedge funds are under consideration and how they might complement the rest of the portfolio.

A growing number of hedge fund analysts believe that most hedge funds do not earn alpha, that is, risk-adjusted returns exceeding a benchmark's returns and that are generated by the manager's skill (see Chapter 3). Instead, the funds earn returns from beta, which is the risk of the market or asset class. Some hedge funds earn this beta by investing in neglected or higher-risk sectors of the investment world. Some use debt to leverage the returns of less risky assets. Separating alpha from beta is not easy in some cases, but hedge fund investors need to understand that earning a high return with lower risk relative to a particular benchmark does not mean that the fund is generating alpha. Instead, investors need to be sure that they are comparing the hedge fund to the correct benchmark or nonhedge fund vehicle.

Despite the potential pitfalls, hedge funds can have their place in some portfolios. Investors who are able to invest in quality hedge funds and who compile a portfolio of complimentary funds can look forward to steadier, less volatile overall return patterns from the portfolio than investors in traditional investment vehicles, and perhaps to higher long-term returns. To achieve these results, the investor must know why he or she is considering hedge funds and how to select funds that are appropriate for that investor.

## Hedge Funds for the Rest of Us

Investors who do not meet the definition of qualified investors or who want to avoid the shortcomings of hedge funds still can reap many of the advantages of hedge funds. A number of mutual funds use strategies that are the same as or similar to classic hedge fund strategies. These mutual funds have no loads and charge reasonable expenses. They also are subject to mutual fund regulations, making more information available to investors about their strategies and holdings. Though some of the hedge fund–like mutual funds are closed to new investors, most are not closed and have minimum investment amounts that make them readily available to many investors. The mutual funds also offer daily liquidity. Their current values can be checked each day in the newspaper or on the Internet, and the funds can be sold with less than a day's notice.

An investor can compile a portfolio of mutual funds that use hedge fund–like strategies, reaping many of the benefits of hedge fund investing while retaining the benefits of mutual fund investing. The key is to select mutual funds that are not highly correlated with the stock market indexes or with each other. Such a portfolio should achieve long-term returns similar to those of the stock indexes with less volatility and fewer periods of steep losses. The portfolio's returns will lag those of the stock indexes during strong equity bull markets but make up that gap at other times.

The following sections present a sampling of mutual funds that use hedge fund investment strategies and that can be combined into a portfolio of hedge fund mutual funds. All were open to new investors at the time this was written.

## Core Hedge Funds

Hussman Strategic Growth has most of its assets invested in a portfolio of about 200 stocks. It then uses options either to hedge the portfolio against a broad market decline or to leverage the portfolio to magnify gains in a market surge. The fund has models of market valuations and market climate it uses to determine the amount of hedging or leverage that is appropriate.

PIMCO All Asset uses valuation models to shift the fund's allocation among different PIMCO mutual funds. PIMCO has mutual funds that invest in a wide range of assets and strategies, allowing the manager to consider most of world's investments and weight the portfolio in the assets the manager finds to be the most undervalued and avoid those that are highly valued. The fund does not have the ability to sell short investments or otherwise profit from a decline in an asset's price.

Leuthold Asset Allocation is similar to PIMCO All Asset in that the portfolio's weight in different assets changes over time based on the valuation models of the manager. Leuthold uses different valuation models than PIMCO. In addition, Leuthold does not consider all the asset classes available to PIMCO. Leuthold will sell short stocks it considers unattractive.

## Long/Short Equity and Market Neutral

A number of mutual funds use these two strategies. Laudus/Rosenberg has several funds, one that focuses on U.S. stocks and another that encompasses global stock markets. Charles Schwab & Co. also has a hedged equity fund using this strategy. This category has more mutual funds than most of the other hedge fund–like mutual funds, but many of the funds in the category are closed to new investors. The Laudus/Rosenberg and Schwab funds use quantitative models that determine the buy and sell decisions.

### Special Situations and Distressed Situations

Several mutual funds engage in these strategies. Third Avenue Value often devotes a large percentage of its portfolio to securities of companies that are in or near bankruptcy or otherwise in financial distress. Berwyn Income also tends to venture into securities of companies in distress in search of high yields and capital gains. FPA Crescent is an unusual balanced fund that will invest in small company stocks and bonds of distressed companies.

The Mutual Series fund family has a history of investing in distressed companies and special situations, but it charges a front-end load since being acquired by the Franklin/Templeton fund group. David Winter, a long-time member of the Mutual Series fund group, created his own mutual fund, Wintergreen fund, that uses the same strategies as the Mutual Series group.

None of these funds invests exclusively in special situations and distressed situations because there are not enough investment opportunities. The rest of their investments tend to be stocks selling at value prices and cash.

## Other Asset Classes

A portfolio of "hedge fund" mutual funds can be rounded out with mutual funds that are not correlated with the equity indexes or with most of the other funds. Funds to consider are those that invest in high-yield bonds, real estate investment trusts, commodities, and international bonds.

## EXPAND THE PORTFOLIO

Peter Bernstein is a long-standing advocate of CAPM, the policy portfolio, and efficient markets. As reported in Chapter 4, Bernstein's advocacy of these positions wavered in the teeth of the 2000–2002 bear market. In a 2003 speech and a follow up newsletter to clients he stated that the fixed policy portfolio should be abandoned.

Bernstein's positions were that investors cannot assume that the future will be like the past, and they must be more flexible. He believed that after the extended bull market, equity investments were likely to produce a period of below-average returns. Locking a portfolio into a large stock position would ensure the investor unsatisfactory returns while retaining the volatility of stocks. Bernstein initially recommended a broader mix of assets in a portfolio. Assets should be purchased that would perform well in different types of markets. In addition to the traditional equity position, there should be hedges against extreme outcomes, such as gold futures, cash, foreign-based investments, inflation-protected bonds, and long-term bonds. The exact allocations in the portfolio would depend on the outlook the investor wanted to adopt and the risks he is willing to take. The recommended portfolio seems to be a less sophisticated version of the All Weather® strategy discussed later in this chapter. (All Weather is a registered trademark of Bridgewater Associates, Inc. All rights reserved.) Implied in Bernstein's recommendation is that, unlike the All Weather strategy, the investor should consider adjusting the allocation over time as forecasts and outlooks change.

Later in 2003, Bernstein modified his views a bit. Bernstein's clients are institutional investors, primarily pension funds and endowments. He recommended that they use some fairly sophisticated techniques such as matching the portfolio mix with the liabilities of the fund and a strategy known as portable alpha. Instead of leaning on the tactical asset allocation that Bernstein appeared to be advocating before, he concluded that investors still should use a fixed policy portfolio. The investor, however, should use the asset and liability matching and portable alpha and perhaps other techniques to reduce the risk of the fixed portfolio in case events do not unfold as anticipated.

The average individual investor can apply this strategy by adding assets that are not in traditional portfolios. These assets might include mutual funds that use hedge fund–like strategies as described earlier. Others assets to be considered are those that do not have the highest long-term returns but that perform well when the rest of the port-folio does not, such as international bonds, commodities, and real estate investment trusts. All of the strategies open to big institutional investors are not open to the individual investor, but the individual can achieve close to the same results and reduce stock market risk by careful selection of mutual funds or other investments with an eye toward achieving true diversification of the portfolio.

The heart of the problem Bernstein addressed is one we already have discussed. A shortcoming of traditional applications of CAPM is that the investor uses asset classes that have long histories and invests in those asset classes with index funds or traditional funds. The returns earned by those assets in any short period are likely to be different from the long-term averages. Returns could be above or below the long-term average. In addition, the assets tend to have fairly high correlations with each other or correlations that fluctuate over time. To avoid the shortcomings of CAPM, investors need to add additional asset classes or use some unconventional strategies, such as changing the allocation periodically or using investment managers that do things differently.

## MANAGE FOR VALUE

Investors can apply their knowledge of the valuation cycle to tradi-tional investments such as mutual funds and stocks. They do not need to invest in vehicles such as the All Weather strategy or hedge funds or even mutual funds with hedge fund strategies. Instead, the portfolio should be constructed and managed with the valuation cycle in mind. Since the valuation cycle in stocks can extend for two decades or longer, an asset's position in the valuation cycle determines the returns an investor in that asset earns over the next decade.

The first step an investor can take is to establish a *core portfolio* of mutual funds. The core portfolio is a fixed allocation of funds that is held for the long term. It is not constructed using CAPM, and index funds are not the preferred holdings. Instead, the most volatile funds and asset classes are excluded from the core portfolio. The extreme price swings of these assets cannot be tolerated by most investors, and the extended bear markets of these assets can make it difficult for the investor to achieve goals if these assets are in the portfolio at the wrong time. Mutual funds that should be excluded from this portfolio include those that invest in U.S. growth stocks, emerging market stocks, high-yield bonds, and commodities. We discuss next how to invest in these investments outside the core portfolio, but to avoid extended periods of high negative returns these investments experience.

The core portfolio should consist of mutual funds whose managers use value investing disciplines. A mutual fund managed with a value strategy allows the investor to capture the long-term returns of an asset class without enduring the worst effects of the pessimist phase of the valuation cycle. Using a mutual fund also means that the investor does not have to determine where an investment is in its valuation cycle. The fund manager is paying attention to valuations and managing the portfolio to avoid the most overvalued assets in the class.

Value funds lag a market index during bull markets, but have higher returns than an index during bear markets or relatively flat markets. Though there is some controversy over the issue, most studies indicate that over the long term and over full market cycles value stock funds earn higher returns than growth stock funds and index funds. Their likelihood of avoiding the largest losses in bear markets is the strongest reason to hold value funds in the core portfolio. The manager of a value fund observes the valuation cycle for that asset class and manages the portfolio to avoid the worst affects of the cycle. Value managers do not completely sell their holdings during the periods of highest valuations, but they are aware that valuations are high and adjust the portfolio to avoid the worst effects of the decline that they know is coming. Some value managers increase their cash holdings when markets seem to be extremely optimistic.

As an example of the benefits of value funds, examine how value stock funds performed in the last phase of the 1990s bull market and the ensuing bear market.

Value stocks had a rough time in the last years of the bull market because, as we have discussed, investors almost exclusively purchased a relatively few large growth company stocks and technology stocks. Once growth stock prices declined sharply, value stock prices began rising. It was only during the period June 2002 through October 2002, when almost all stocks declined, that the bear market finally took its toll on value stock funds.

During this period, the performance of some of the value stock funds—recommended in my newsletter *Retirement Watch*—is shown in Table 6.1. The Vanguard 500 Index is used as the market benchmark for comparison. The table shows that all of the value funds earned solid returns during the last leg of the bull market, though they lagged the historic high returns of the market index. Each of the value funds did significantly better than the index during both the entire bear market and the first phase of the bear market. There are differences among the returns of the value funds; but all did significantly better than the index.

**TABLE 6.1**   Comparison of Value Stock Funds

| Fund | 1998–2000* | 2000–2002* | 1998–2002* |
|---|---|---|---|
| Dodge & Cox Stock | 27.03 | 30.58 | 44.13 |
| American Century Equity Income | 11.81 | 40.27 | 45.41 |
| Torray | 31.65 | 1.20 | 12.16 |
| Third Avenue Value | 37.73 | 10.42 | 23.46 |
| S&P 500 | 59.22 | −26.89 | −3.00 |

* Total returns are for January 1, 1998, through March 31, 2000; April 1, 2000, through May 31, 2000; and January 1, 1998, through December 31, 2002.

In the period from June 2002 to October 2002, all stocks and mutual funds sharply declined, including the value funds. The 1998–2002 period essentially is a market cycle, though not a long-term or secular cycle. The market index basically ended the period where it began, giving investors in it a small loss. Yet the value funds had strong total returns for the period.

Value funds are not without risk. Because each fund invests in a particular asset class, it carries some of the risk of that class. The risk is reduced, however, because the manager pays attention to the valuation cycle within its investment mandate. The value fund will have less risk, perhaps much less risk, than the index.

The core portfolio should follow the basic diversification principles of MPT. There should be a collection of funds that invest in asset classes or use investment styles that are not highly correlated with each other. The exact portfolio depends on the returns the investor seeks and the level of volatility the investor is willing to take. A solid, simple core portfolio would include one or more funds from each of these classes; U.S. large company stocks, U.S. small company stocks, developed market international stocks, real estate stocks, a U.S. bond fund, and an international bond fund. The value investor also might want to include one or more of the "hedge fund" mutual funds in the portfolio.

Why should an investor own a core portfolio at all? Why have any permanent holdings if it is known that there will be times, perhaps extended periods, when a fund will be in a bear market?

As demonstrated earlier in this chapter, there is not a reliable way to determine in advance or even in the early stages the tops and bottoms of the valuation cycle. The bias of the economy and most markets is toward growth and appreciation. While it is desirable to avoid loss periods entirely, there also is a risk to being out of a market during bull markets. In the U.S. stock market in particular, gains for any particular year tend to be packed into a few days. An investor who is out of the market for the best days of each year will not earn most of the long-term appreciation of the stock markets. In fact, an investor who misses the best few days of the stock market each year is likely to earn no more than short-term Treasury bills. Owning a value fund all the time is a good way to balance the risk of potential bear market losses and the lost opportunity from being out of the market during its best days.

An investor might want to own only a core portfolio. The only work required of the investor is to rebalance the portfolio periodically (such as annually) to bring the funds back to their original allocation and to replace any funds that have major structural changes. Some investors, however, might want to be more active in response to the valuation cycle. They might want to seize opportunities in assets that are in the phase of extreme pessimism or reduce holdings of assets that are in the phase of extreme optimism.

For these investors, the core portfolio can be complemented by a *managed portfolio.*

The managed portfolio begins with the same asset allocation as the core portfolio; but over time the holdings in the managed portfolio change with the valuation cycles of different assets. As an asset appears to reach high valuations, its position in the portfolio is reduced or eliminated. Assets that appear to be at low valuations or even fair valuations have positions added or increased. The advantage of having a managed portfolio is that at times the highly volatile assets that are not recommended for the core portfolio can be added. For example, when growth stocks or emerging market stocks are selling at low relative valuations, they can be added to the managed portfolio. The risk of suffering substantial losses from such holdings is reduced, because the asset is not in the phase of extreme optimism. This approach to investing allows the investor to capture a high percentage of the long-term gains of an asset class while avoiding most of the periods of high losses that are incurred by buy-and-hold investors.

In line with what we have learned from Rational Beliefs Theory and other sources, managed portfolio changes should not made using methods that could be considered day trading or short-term trading. The investor has two choices for making decisions. The investor can observe the cyclical bull and bear markets. This means assets would be added to or subtracted from this portfolio using a one- to three-year time frame. Or the investor can follow the long-term, or secular, valuation cycle and make even less frequent changes.

The difficulty the managed portfolio presents for the investor is determining when to make changes. As we learned earlier in this chapter, there is not one or even a small number of reliable indicators or statistics that can be used to identify when an asset should be added to or subtracted from the portfolio. Attempting to use mechanical or automatic investment signals will result in disappointment. Instead, the investor will have to look at a broad range of investment data and market trends to make decisions.

Ultimately, the managed portfolio investor should remember that the key to investment success is to avoid large losses. The investor should look at the available investment assets, try to identify the risks in each, and then ask the questions: Which risks do I want to avoid? Which risks am I willing to take? Assets with risks the investor wants to avoid should be sold or reduced. Assets with risks the investor is willing to take should be purchased or increased. While the managed portfolio administered in this way should earn above average returns, the idea is not to seek the next hot investment or mutual fund. Instead, the goal should be to reduce risk by limiting exposure to investments that seem overvalued and at risk of tumbling. Eliminating the high-risk assets and seeking those with lower risk automatically avoids the likely big losers. It also positions the portfolio in the assets that are most likely to do well over the next few years. The strategy reduces the risk and volatility of the portfolio.

The managed portfolio strategy is close to a strategy called *Tactical Asset Allocation*. TAA was widely used by institutional investors before the bull market of the 1990s made buy-and-hold investing appear to be the better route. In addition, most TAA strategies used one or a few data points to make portfolio adjustments. The efficacy of those signals declined over time, as happens with all such indicators. Portfolio adjustments described here should be guided by data and a study of the data's history. But judgment ultimately must guide the decisions. Investors also should remember that the primary goal of the portfolio changes is risk reduction, not seeking the highest returns.

## THE ALL WEATHER STRATEGY

Ray Dalio had a problem. He was the founder of a successful money management firm for institutional investors, such as pension funds. He had established plans and trust funds for his loved ones, and he was managing the assets. But he worried what would happen to these funds in the future. Dalio had seen and heard of too many cases in which inherited funds were taken over by new trustees or money managers who subsequently lost a large share of the wealth. He sought a way of ensuring that the wealth would be preserved for his loved ones.

Because of his role as a money manager for sophisticated institutional investors, Dalio had considerable resources at his firm upon which he could draw. To solve his problem, Dalio and his firm, Bridgewater Associates, created the All Weather strategy. The goal of the strategy is to generate consistent, high returns across a wide variety of economic and market environments with few adjustments. In other words, the strategy as a whole is designed to be relatively immune from the wide fluctuations caused by the valuation cycles in different asset classes, especially stocks.

Bridgewater began its process using CAPM, but it modified CAPM in several ways. As we know from an earlier chapter, most users of CAPM study historical data to conclude that stocks have the highest long-term returns. This data cause them to construct portfolios with large allocations to stocks. Bridgewater concluded that nominal long-term returns are not the best measure to use when considering assets for a long-term portfolio. Instead, returns after adjusting for risk were the relevant metric. Bridgewater's study indicated other asset classes that are less volatile than stocks generate risk-adjusted returns that are the same or similar to those of stocks. In addition, the risk and return of an asset can be raised or lowered by using leverage, either increasing or decreasing those qualities. For most financial assets, leverage is available through futures and options contracts instead of through debt.

Most investors assign a single long-term value to each element: risk, return, and correlation. Those values are used to determine the proper diversification. For the All Weather strategy, Bridgewater concluded that performance under different economic conditions was the appropriate measurement period. The goal is to own assets that do not have correlated valuation cycles so that the investor will not experience extended periods of below-average returns in almost any economic environment. Bridgewater determined that two factors determine the direction of most investments over any meaningful period: economic growth and inflation. Either of these factors can be rising or falling, making four potential economic environments to be managed: rising growth, falling growth, rising inflation, and falling inflation. Of course, two of these are likely to happen at any time. But for purposes of constructing the strategy, the environments could be considered separately.

Bridgewater decided to balance assets that do well in these different environments. Investments that do well in the different environments would each be allowed 25 percent of the strategy's risk. For example, investments that do well in a rising economy would be weighted so that they comprise 25 percent of the risk of the strategy, measured by the standard deviation or volatility. So, instead of comparing the correlations of the investments directly with each other, the All Weather strategy correlates the investments with the different economic environments. The result should be a collection of assets that have strong returns and poor returns at different times and in different economic environments. One or more groups of the assets should be in a bull market while another group or more of assets will be in a bear market. If correlations are determined properly and uncorrelated assets are balanced, the value will not fluctuate as much as that of a portfolio that is tilted toward stocks or some other asset. The strategy will not be subject to long periods of below average returns when stocks are in a secular bear market. Such extended bear markets can crimp the lifestyles of those dependent on the strategy, especially if the bear markets coincide with the peak spending years of the dependents. The strategy also is not likely to have extended periods of very high returns when stocks are in a bull market, but over the long-term, the risk-adjusted return should be close to that of an equity-tilted portfolio.

The All Weather strategy has assets that are not readily available to the typical individual investor and some, in fact, are not traditionally considered investment asset classes.

The assets that do well when economic growth is rising are equities, corporate/mortgage spreads, emerging market debt spreads, and commodities. Corporate/mortgage spreads are the differences between yields or interest rates on treasury bonds and those on corporate bonds and mortgages. This investment is captured using financial derivatives, such as futures and options, usually by buying one type of bond and selling short the other. Likewise, emerging market debt spreads are the yield difference between U.S. Treasury bonds and bonds issued by emerging market countries.

Investments that do well when inflation is rising are inflation-linked, or inflation-indexed, bonds issued around the globe, not only U.S. inflation-indexed bonds. Also included are commodities and the emerging market debt spreads. Only two assets are in the group that does well when economic growth is falling: nominal bonds and inflation-linked bonds. Nominal bonds are traditional bonds that have no inflation adjustment. They can include both government and corporate bonds (though Bridgewater uses only government bonds in the strategy). The group of assets that do well when inflation is falling also has only two members: nominal bonds and equities.

Despite its name, the All Weather strategy does not preserve its value in all economic environments. In periods of rising short-term interest rates and credit reduction, such as when the Federal Reserve is tightening monetary policy, all the assets tend to decline to some extent. So the strategy does have periods when it incurs losses. Also, the strategy can decline over short periods such as a month or quarter. In most economic environments and over extended periods, however, some of the assets will rise and others will fall. The periods when all the assets are declining are likely to be much shorter and have lower losses than for a traditional portfolio derived using CAPM.

Bridgewater stands ready to adjust the allocations if a fundamental change appears to have occurred in the correlations. In addition, assets can be added or subtracted as the choices in the financial markets change.

The All Weather strategy as Bridgewater constructs it is not available to most investors. Bridgewater works only with pension funds and other institutional investors. Some of the asset classes, such as the corporate/mortgage spreads, are not something the average investor can purchase. Also, leverage is used to adjust the strategy to the desired level of risk, not something that the average investor or his advisors does as a matter of course.

Yet the All Weather strategy is instructive to every investor.

The strategy has important improvements to CAPM. The method does seek the highest return for a given level of risk. Yet, it does not use long-term returns and correlations of the assets to each other to determine the appropriate asset mix. Instead, the strategy looks at how assets perform in different economic environments and their correlations with those environments. This recognition of market cycles and different economic environments is an improvement to CAPM that is more likely to achieve the long-term goals of investors and reduce the probability of extended periods of losses or below-average returns.

Investors can use this approach to construct better portfolios using the traditional assets available to them. They cannot implement the full All Weather strategy. They will, however, have less volatile portfolios than the traditional CAPM portfolios.

## THE RISK MANAGER

Which portfolios and portfolio management strategies will deliver the returns an investor needs to generate sufficient real (after inflation) cash flow for life?

The goal of almost any investor can be expressed in terms of having sufficient cash in the future for a specific expense or series of expenses. Whether that goal is met depends on the investment strategy used by the investor and the point in its valuation cycle or investment regime each asset in the portfolio is in.

The investment markets are riskier than acknowledged by most investment theories. Those risks often are washed out in the very long-term, but investors operate in shorter periods. The objective of the investor is to identify and manage the risks of the world's investment markets. Because markets and the economy change, an investor's goals are more likely to be achieved when the investor has the adaptability and flexibility of a fox. A hedgehog investor's goals are met only if the one big thing that investor believes is consistent with the secular market trends of the time.

Long-term investment success—investing like a fox—boils down to two key actions: manage risks and be willing to be different. The main risk to an investor is in assets that are moving from periods of extreme optimism to extreme pessimism in their valuation cycles. At that point, most investors already own such assets and are optimistic about them. An investor's portfolio and its strategy must be different from that of most investors if he or she is to avoid a period of below-average returns or even significant losses.

# CHAPTER 7

# ADVICE FOR FOXES AND HEDGEHOGS

## Key Investment Mistakes to Avoid

What an investor thinks is less important than how the investor thinks. Having an adaptable, flexible outlook is more important than having certain beliefs about what causes changes in the prices of different investments. We learned this counterintuitive concept in Chapter 1 and have developed it throughout this book.

A concept the reader also might have grasped from the discussion is that in general a good investor is one who acts counterintuitively. One reason many investors earn disappointing returns is that the actions they need to take often are the opposite of the actions they want to take and feel comfortable taking. A benefit of the Capital Asset Pricing Model (CAPM) is that it keeps investors from making some classic mistakes. CAPM's emphasis on a buy-and-hold portfolio and on almost scientific calculations of return and risk limit the scope of actions an investor takes. CAPM makes some false assumptions, which were discussed in previous chapters. But one of the reasons CAPM became popular was that it kept investors from routinely taking some actions that led to unsatisfactory returns.

An investor who thinks like a fox and recognizes the valuation cycle avoids some of the negative effects of CAPM and other hedgehog strategies. But the foxlike investor puts himself at risk of taking some actions that can increase risk or reduce returns. Other investors also are prone to making these mistakes.

Fortunately, an entire school of thought has sprung up to study the mistakes investors routinely make and caution them against making these mistakes in the future. This school, now known as *Behavioral Finance*, won a share of the 2002 Nobel Prize for economics in the person of psychologist Daniel Kahnemann. Perhaps not surprisingly Behavioral Finance originated outside of the finance and economics departments of universities. It began with psychologists and social scientists studying human behavior. Unlike other branches of investment and finance, this one did not start with a theory or an attempt to construct a theory. Instead, Behavioral Finance began with studies of human behavior in different situations. Only over time did people realize that the findings could be applied to improve money management, and finance academics and professionals began their own studies in the field. Behavioral Finance findings now are used to design 401(k) plans and to educate investors. Some adherents have broadened the studies to examine managerial business decisions and identify mistakes executives routinely make.

Advocates of CAPM and other branches of finance argue that Behavioral Finance is not an investment philosophy or theory. They are correct. Behavioral Finance identifies traits and habits that make people prone to commit investment and financial mistakes. It focuses on individual actions and to some extent on how they affect the markets. Behavioral Finance does not give an investor a strategy for constructing a portfolio or allocating assets. Behavioral Finance also does not give investors many instructions on actions to take. Instead, the studies identify mistakes people make with their money and advises investors not to take those actions.

The lessons learned from Behavioral Finance can be applied profitably by investors using broader investment theories that do focus on asset allocation and other key elements of constructing a portfolio. The findings of Behavioral Finance can be beneficial to fox-like investors whose investment strategies recognize Rational Beliefs Theory and the *valuation cycle*. Investors who make periodic adjustments to their portfolios are those most at risk of making the mistakes identified by Behavioral Finance.

The actions identified by Behavioral Finance are made so frequently that many believe they are hard-wired into human beings by either evolution or generations of learning. Neurologists even have joined in the studies by examining with MRIs and other devices the brains of individuals while they make decisions. Some theorists have concluded that the same part of the brain that controls the "fight or flight" emotion also takes over from the analytic parts of the brain when it is time to make some financial decisions. For example, when the stocks in a portfolio have declined steadily for a while, an investor's emotions press him to sell all stocks to avoid further losses. A long-term study of stock behavior would tell the investor that the sale is likely to be at or near the bottom of a cycle, and the stock prices should rise at some point. But the defensive tendencies that have developed in humans over generations are likely to treat the portfolio decline the same as a personal attack and urge the investor to save the rest of the portfolio by selling. A related finding, from a field some are calling *neuroeconomics*, is that people with damage to the part of the brain that controls the ability to experience emotions such as fear do better at an investment game than people without the damage.

The key for the investor is to recognize the tendencies identified by Behavioral Finance. With that awareness, the investor either can learn to avoid the actions or can set up safeguards in his or her investment strategy that minimize the risk of making the mistakes.

We already have discussed some of these findings in other contexts, and the readers should recognize them as they are presented again. Behavioral Finance begins by rejecting a basic assumption of CAPM and conventional investment theory—that investors are perfectly rational actors. Rational Beliefs already accepted the notion that investors make mistakes. Behavioral Finance has developed the point further; different types of mistakes have been identified, labeled, and defined. These different mistakes also can be placed into four broad categories, and that is how we will look at them in this chapter. Some researchers group the traits differently (or do not group them at all). Others use different labels or combine two or more of these actions into one. The format used here is that used by Max Bazerman of the Harvard Business School in *Judgment in Managerial Decision Making* (Hoboken, NJ: John Wiley & Sons, 2006).

## MISPERCEPTIONS AND ILLUSIONS

Perhaps all the findings of Behavioral Finance can be put under this heading. For now, we place only three actions directly under it.

One of the early discoveries of Behavioral Finance was *anchoring* or, as it is also called, *myopia*. Investors often will take a recent event or one with which they have long been familiar and assume that all similar events will have the same outcome. They will not consider ways in which subsequent events are different from the first one or the possibility that the outcome of the first event was caused by factors the investor is not even considering.

We have discussed variants of this behavior, particularly in regard to investors' finding patterns in data when there really are not any. Investors need to resist the temptation to conclude there is a cause and effect relationship between events until they have done a thorough, careful study and considered alternative explanations.

Another classic trait is called *hindsight bias*. After an event has occurred, a person will exclaim, "I knew it." Occasionally, a person actually is on record as having forecast the series of events or result. More often, the true progression of events is as follows. An investor mentions a stock or mutual fund and perhaps adds it to the portfolio. The investment's price increases considerably. The investor then claims to have known in advance that the investment would rise by that amount and why. More often, the truth is the investor had no notion the return would be as high as it was and events occurred to propel the increase of which the investor had no idea. This bias also can work in the opposite direction, with the investor claiming to have known that a bad investment would indeed generate losses and why.

A danger of hindsight bias is that it prevents an investor from recognizing mistakes, even from investment decisions that earned good returns. Investors can make mistakes on profitable investments, a form of doing the right thing for the wrong reason. The investor needs to consider this possibility and make a dispassionate comparison of the reasons the investment acted the way it did with his expectations at the time the investment was purchased. Otherwise, he could make the same mistake in the future and have less profitable results.

Hindsight bias can have two other adverse effects. It can give an investor a false confidence in his ability (which Behavioral Finance says already is common among investors). Hindsight bias also can lead the investor to make false conclusions about what caused the gains or losses, and those false conclusions can influence future investment decisions and lead to losses.

Hindsight bias is one reason many professional investors commit to writing their reasons for buying or selling an investment. Rather than relying on faulty memory or hindsight bias, they want to know exactly what they understood before the investment was purchased. They want to compare the actual events to those they forecast. It might be true that it is better to be lucky than good, but it is important to know whether one has been lucky or good.

Another common trait is *positive illusions,* or perennial optimism. This trait can occur on several levels. Some investors have positive illusions about every investment in their portfolios. Once money has been put in an investment, the investor loses the ability to analyze it objectively. All changes are viewed positively, even if they contradict the reasons for the initial purchase. On broader levels, an investor can be unduly bullish about either a particular asset class or most markets, or the investor can have unwarranted optimism about his or her investment prowess.

Any of these types of positive illusions hamper the ability to make a realistic analysis and effective investment decisions. An investor who studies Rational Beliefs Theory and recognizes that the valuation cycle exists for all investments is less likely to be perennially optimistic. The difficulty for the investor, as we will see later in this chapter, is that other tendencies are to be risk averse and to avoid uncertainty. These are errors in the opposite direction and can cause an investor to invest too conservatively. An investor needs to balance the tendencies to be perennially optimistic on the one hand and risk averse on the other.

## MEASUREMENT ERRORS

These are mistakes that we have reviewed or hinted at elsewhere in the book and are very common even among professional investors and analysts. There are different ways investors can misinterpret data and draw erroneous conclusions.

*Sample-size error* is common in the investment world because public investment markets are a relatively new development in human history and are evolving. We do not have a sufficient amount of reliable data from which to draw conclusions for many aspects of investing. That does not stop people from trying.

A classic example of sample size error is to tie the presidential election cycle to the stock market. While there does appear to be a correlation indicating that the best years for the stock market are the third years of presidential terms, and especially the third years of second terms, there have not been enough occurrences under the modern stock markets to say the conclusions are statistically reliable. The theory is interesting and worth further study, but the sample size is too small to be a basis for investing significant amounts of capital. (This also can be an example of anchoring.) Some analysts actually label this trait superstitious behavior because the investor is acting on little more than the observation that at some point in the past this behavior was followed by a reward.

Another sampling-size error, which is a prime cause of the valuation cycle, is to *ignore regression to the mean*. Investors tend to believe that recent results that are either above or below average are likely to continue indefinitely. We know from our discussions earlier in this book that such beliefs are wrong. It helps cause the correlation of beliefs and persistence of beliefs that lead to the extreme optimism and extreme pessimism phases of the valuation cycle.

A complicated label for a simple concept is *conjunctive* and *disjunctive* events bias. Certain events must occur for a particular outcome to be realized. For example, inflation must decline for interest rates to fall, and that often leads to stronger economic growth and higher stock prices. Investors tend to *mis*estimate the likelihood of the triggering event or events occurring and leading to the ultimate outcome. Some people are biased toward believing the negative events will occur, while others are biased toward the positive events.

Researchers found an interesting twist in this error. When several events all must occur to achieve an outcome, people tend to overestimate the probability that all of them will occur. Yet when they focus on the probability of only one needed event occurring, investors tend to underestimate the probability that it will occur.

This is an important error for investors to fight against because estimating the probability of events occurring is a key to good risk management of a portfolio.

## RISK-TAKING BIASES

Anyone who has worked with individual investors learns quickly that most people have tendencies and biases that are contrary to good investment decision making. That is why I said earlier that most good investing decisions are counterintuitive. People tend to avoid actions that will make them uncomfortable, even for relatively brief periods of time. Yet markets are filled with uncertainty and the unknown. It is difficult to earn acceptable returns or reduce risk without venturing outside one's comfort zone.

*Regret avoidance* is an emotion we all have seen in many different contexts. People tend to feel more regret over actions taken than they do over actions not taken. After an investment is purchased, many buyers are uncomfortable with the decision; they have difficulty living with it even if it turns out well. But if a person does not act, he feels less regret even if the decision foregone would have been a good one. Apparently, this occurs because the lack of a decision means there is no commitment, but there still is the possibility of making a decision in the future. The decision made and action taken causes more turmoil than the action not taken.

One of the early discoveries of Behavioral Finance is called *loss aversion* or *asymmetry of risk tolerance*. Briefly stated, people tend to feel the pain of losses more than they enjoy the satisfaction of gains of an equal amount. Because of this trait, people take actions that are the opposite of the actions they should take. Standard investment advice is to let one's gains run and cut one's losses. Instead, many investors will sell a winning investment soon after it produces a paper gain so that they can lock in the gain. When an investment loses money, investors will vow to hold the asset until it at least returns to their purchase price, if it ever does.

The wiser course is, before buying an investment, to determine to sell automatically if it declines more than a certain percentage or if adverse news occurs that the investor was not expecting. The individual should set the maximum loss that will be tolerated and sell if the asset declines beyond that point. Then, the investor can dispassionately reanalyze the investment.

An understandable trait but one that reduces returns is avoiding uncertainty. Uncertainty is a permanent feature of the markets. The need for certainty causes investors to make three different mistakes.

Many investors are too conservative because they have that trait for loss aversion. Despite the need for gains that will at least exceed inflation and taxes, too many investors select the most conservative investments for the bulk of their portfolios because they are afraid of incurring any losses, even those that they realize are likely to be temporary due to market cycles. Sponsors of 401(k) plans frequently find that even their youngest employees are so averse to risk and uncertainty that their accounts are invested in money market funds or stable value funds. Instead, investors should study market history and valuation cycles to understand the risks of the markets and how to minimize them without trying to eliminate them. Younger investors, in particular, should realize that time is the best tool for reducing uncertainty.

Another mistake caused by avoiding uncertainty is that investors become attracted to the arguments of analysts who speak or write with more certainty than others. Instead of evaluating the arguments themselves, the investors evaluate the manner in which the arguments and especially the conclusions are presented. An analyst who recommends an investment but also fully discusses the risks and uncertainty involved in the recommendation will likely fail to persuade these investors.

Some people avoid uncertainty because they have *compromised self-efficacy*. In personal finance, this means the individual professes not to understand money or the markets and believes that all attempts to increase understanding are futile. The investor believes that financial outcomes will be negative despite whatever efforts are made to improve financial decisions. There is then little reason to put real effort into financial decisions or even to make decisions.

Stubbornness is not a term that finds it way into research papers; so it is called *internal escalation of commitment*. It simply means that once a decision is made, an investor tends to become more firmly convinced over time that the decision was correct. In the worst instances, the investor either ignores information that is contrary to the decision or finds ways to interpret the information to favor the decision.

*Competitive escalation* is another behavior that occurs in the extreme optimism phase of the valuation cycle. Investors who have stayed out of an asset, after having seen the price increase and others make high returns, decide to join the crowd and hope the price rise continues. This occurs on a smaller scale near the end of each calendar quarter as money managers who are underperforming their benchmarks buy investments that have been leading the market.

## DECISION-MAKING BIAS

People like to think that they are making careful, well-researched decisions. Yet many people have internal biases they are not aware of that influence their research and the way they make decisions. Those biases can lead to poor decisions.

*Availability* describes a trait in which people make decisions based on the most recent information available to them or on the most vivid information available to them.

A good example of this involves *real estate investment trusts* (REITS). They had a checkered history in the 1970s. Major banks formed REITs mainly as vehicles for making more real estate loans and capturing the fees. The REITs were not well managed, made poor property purchases, and borrowed too much. Investors in those early REITs had poor returns. Then the industry changed during the 1980s. Investors who purchased REITs during the late 1980s or early 1990s, when property prices were depressed, scored significant gains afterward. Nevertheless, many investors based their opinion of REITs on the headlines from the earlier years and missed the opportunity.

A widespread trait in the investment world is labeled *irretrievabil-ity.* This is when an investor is unable to think beyond a preconceived notion. For example, some investors believe that a stock split always is positive for a stock and a good reason to buy. Research does not support the idea, and it is clear that a stock split does not change any of a company's fundamentals. Yet the rule is fairly widely accepted. Many such beliefs are widely held, though careful study refutes them. Investors simply have trouble dismissing an idea they have held, especially if others also hold the idea.

Another decision-making error is *presuming associations.* Investors assume that certain associations exist in the markets though there is no real evidence to support the idea. For example, many investors believe that a price-earnings ratio in excess of 20 for a major index is an indication that stocks are overvalued and due for a significant decline. In fact, a study of the markets shows that a P/E ratio in excess of 20 leads to below average returns only over an extended period of 10 years. Over shorter periods, the momentum gathered in the markets continues after the multiple exceeds 20. The indexes earn above average returns for the following one, three, and five years.

Investors frequently search for validation of decisions that they have made, falling into the *validation trap.* Often unconsciously, the investor searches for information that confirms the decision was a good one and also interprets new information in ways that affirm the wisdom of the decision. If an investor has decided that inflation will rise, the investor is likely to see indications of rising prices in everyday life and to search for signs of rising inflation in the data. Once a decision is made, the investor loses the ability to continue evaluating it impartially and becomes emotionally committed to the initial decision.

In some versions of validation, the investor will look to the actions of others who are perceived to be similar or in a similar situation.

The investor will attempt to duplicate the decisions of those people. The danger is that the role models might not be as similar as the investor imagines. The decisions they are making could be wrong for the investor. In addition, this process assumes that the role models are making good decisions. They could be making poor, uninformed decisions that will be harmful to them and to those who imitate them.

There are some other investor traits discovered by Behavioral Finance that are not in Bazerman's framework.

*Overconfidence* is another early finding of Behavioral Finance. Investors simply are more confident in their judgment and ability than they should be. Overconfidence leads an investor to trade too often, skimp on research, fail to diversify, and eschew consulting experts. Overconfidence also leads the investor to hindsight bias and other mistakes discussed in this chapter.

Related to overconfidence is the *illusion of control.* In a wide variety of tasks, people have an illusion of control over events. Researchers have studied people in many different activities, including tasks as random as coin tossing, and found that people tended to believe they were influencing events and that they had above average skill. The studies show that people are more likely to believe they are in control when there are a number of available choices, they have early success, the task is familiar, the amount of available information is high, and they are personally involved. These factors describe investing for many people. Investors can fight the illusion that they have control by focusing on risk control and keeping a written record of why they made investment decisions.

Another related trait is *self-attribution bias,* where people protect their self-esteem. Not surprisingly, people generally attribute successes to their own ability and skill most of the time. Losses and other adverse results most often are attributed to bad luck or other forces outside the individual's control. The problem with this thinking is that it eliminates the ability of people to learn from their mistakes because they do not believe they made mistakes.

All of these traits might be part of what is called *feedback distortion*. When people receive feedback on their decisions or actions, they frequently are able to distort the feedback so that it reflects positively on their abilities.

*Polarized thinking* is another behavior that can reduce investment returns. The polarized thinker is one who thinks without shades of gray. An investment is either good or bad, meaning that the investor either should own a lot of it or none of it. The markets are not this black and white. That is why portfolios should be diversified. The markets have far less certainty and more risk than the polarized thinker believes. Without some change in this investor's outlook, the portfolio is likely to be highly concentrated.

*Mental accounting* is a trait that pervades personal financial decisions. People tend to concentrate on parts of their portfolios or finances and view each part in its own box. In other words, each item is put in its own mental account. These investors do not look at the portfolio as a whole or consider how a decision affects the entire portfolio.

Consider the essential practice of diversification. A properly diversified portfolio has assets with low correlations to each other. In a simple two-asset portfolio, one asset should be rising while the other is declining or holding steady. The investor who engages in mental accounting focuses on the poorer-performing asset, sells it, and increases the allocation to the asset that is rising in price. Mental accounting leads to the loss of diversification and its benefits.

Mental accounting also leads an investor to focus only on one element of an investment such as returns. We learned earlier in this book that risk management is at least as important as potential returns. An investor who focuses only on returns ignores the level of risk in the portfolio, the volatility of the portfolio's returns, or how the portfolio is likely to perform if the investment environment changes.

Many of the mistakes that Behavioral Finance identified can be attributed fully or partially to one cause. The cause is what the scholars call heuristics and what regular people call shortcuts. People, especially investors, love mental shortcuts. It is comforting to believe that someone somewhere carefully researched history and theory and concluded that one or more simple rules dictate the correct investment actions. Investors also gain a sense of authority by knowing shortcuts or rules of thumb they can turn to when a decision needs to be made or portfolios are under discussion.

The traits identified by Behavioral Finance tend to be self-destructive to the investor. If unchecked, they lead to poor portfolio decisions, reduced returns, and higher risk. There are several steps an investor can take to avoid having a portfolio affected by these behaviors.

• An investor who is aware of the behaviors identified by Behavioral Finance and why they lead to bad decisions is more likely to recognize them if they creep into his or her own portfolio process. A study of the findings of Behavioral Finance can help improve investment performance.

• Another effective step is to avoid making portfolio decisions when feeling emotional. One of the key findings of Behavioral Finance is that the bulk of these actions occur when an investor is allowing emotions to dominate decisions. The investor needs to establish a process to ensure that investments are influenced more by research and a careful process than by emotions.

• Education is a key element to avoiding the adverse actions discussed in this chapter. Careful research will reduce the instances when investment decisions are made using rules of thumb, short-cuts, logical fallacies, or the emotion-controlling parts of the brain. None of us can ever become the perfectly rational investor assumed in the Efficient Market Hypothesis, but we can avoid many of the traits discovered by Behavioral Finance.

• Make a written record of why an investment was purchased and which events should cause a sale. The sell rules should be followed once developed. Following the sell rules will ensure that a losing investment will not be retained because an investor is unwilling to recognize a loss. The investor will not make emotional mistakes such as seeking confirmation of the decision in all available news. A written record before a purchase also makes it less likely that an investment will be purchased simply because it is rising or the investor knows others who are buying it.

The written record makes it easier for the investor to abide by the long-term plan. Many investors fall for the behavioral pitfalls because they do not have a guide that will keep them from the influences of the latest news and hype.

• Focusing on the big picture also is a key to avoiding behavioral mistakes. Poor performance in one asset for a short time will not result in action if the investor understands that it was placed in the portfolio for its long-term diversification benefits. A long-term focus also will not cause an investor to change the portfolio when investors as a whole allow current news or individual pieces of data to influence their outlook. An investor who has studied the markets and focused on the big picture will have a good understanding of which data have a lasting influence on the markets and which theories are myths.

The easiest way to avoid the mental mistakes most investors make is to remember the simple rule that the right investment decision often is the counterintuitive move. In many activities it makes sense to believe what most others do, follow widely believed rules of thumb, or go with what has worked best in the recent past. But such actions often lead to disappointing investment returns. Remembering this simple idea can help an investor avoid the mistakes that are widespread in the investment markets.

# CHAPTER 8

# PORTFOLIOS OF THE FUTURE

The investment management business is dynamic. I observed many changes in the business during the more than 15 years that I have served as a trustee for a local government pension fund in Virginia. Most of the firms we review, and especially their personnel, are dramatically different from their counterparts of less than two decades ago. The changes also are reflected in the portfolios they construct and strategies they employ. There definitely are trends in these changes, and these trends indicate what portfolios of the future will look like.

A few years ago the education background of a portfolio manager often was unspectacular and virtually irrelevant. Occasionally, a manager had a master's in business administration or some other advanced degree, but the usual background was a four-year degree in a nonbusiness program. Even when the college degree was in a business-related program, it often was unrelated to investments or finance. Portfolio managers generally learned their trade through on-the-job training that almost amounted to an apprenticeship system. A future portfolio manager often began as a bank lending officer, a credit analyst at an insurance company, or a stock or bond analyst at an investment firm. In each case, the novice learned from senior employees how to evaluate companies and markets. Over time, the employee would be given more and more responsibility until, for those who proved themselves capable, they became portfolio managers or even started their own investment management firms.

More recently, the education and career path changed at many firms. Investment professionals and portfolio managers often have advanced degrees. More and more of these degrees are in business-related programs, and many hold the certified financial analyst (CFA) designation. In recent years more and more of the advanced degrees are in mathematics, statistics, physics, and other fields with a heavy emphasis on mathematics. The degrees often are doctorates. There even are nuclear scientists helping to select investments at a number of firms. Holders of these degrees have little or no experience as analysts, lending officers, or similar traditional positions. Usually, they moved directly from the academic world to investment firms. Some began their careers in jobs more relevant to their education, then realized that their skills could be used in investment management in work they found both more interesting and more lucrative.

Recall from Chapter 3 that quantitative analysis and computers became critical to investment strategies with the development of Modern Portfolio Theory (MPT) and the Capital Asset Pricing Model (CAPM). CAPM and the Efficient Market Hypothesis (EMH) maintain that traditional fundamental analysis of companies is a futile exercise; investors cannot exceed the returns of a market index through stock selection. Acceptance of this hypothesis led a number of investment firms away from traditional investment analysis. The new theories also introduced new ways of analyzing investments and markets that include mathematics-based concepts such as alpha, beta, $r$-squared, the Sharpe ratio, and more. The new breed of portfolio managers and analysts went to work evaluating portfolios and investment opportunities using these new tools. Many of this new breed of investment managers and analysts say that they know little or nothing about the businesses or economic fundamentals of the companies whose stocks and bonds they buy.

More importantly, the choices available in the investment world changed. Analyzing the new investments and incorporating them into a portfolio require different skills. These new investments play a more important role in portfolios now and that role will increase over time.

Just a few decades ago, most investors were limited to the simple option of buying and selling stocks and bonds. This simple world is complicated enough, because there are many stocks and bonds to evaluate. A few venturesome investors also would sell short some stocks. But even individual and institutional investors, who were considered sophisticated, generally limited their portfolios to stocks, bonds, and some real estate. There are only a few ways to increase returns or limit losses within that investment spectrum. The selection of individual securities to buy is one tool available to the portfolio manager. Changing the allocation between stocks, bonds, and real estate is another strategy. The portfolio manager also can reduce both stocks and bonds and increase the amount of cash or near-cash assets.

Most traditional portfolio managers are given specific investment assignments, usually limiting the assets that can be purchased. A manager might be limited to large-capitalization stocks in the United States, small-capitalization U.S. stocks, or emerging market stocks, for example. In these cases, the portfolio manager cannot buy bonds or other assets or increase cash above a certain level. Such traditional approaches are known as "long-only" portfolios, because the investor's only option is to purchase securities with the expectation of selling them at a higher price. The manager cannot sell securities short, use alternative assets, enhance returns with options or futures, hedge the portfolio, or take other nontraditional actions.

Today, most portfolios still are long-only, even among pension funds and other institutions. There are a growing number of portfolios, however, that use a broader range of strategies. These portfolios contain assets other than conventional securities and might contain no conventional securities. These portfolios can earn positive returns when the indexes against which long-only portfolios are measured are generating negative returns. In the future, more and more portfolios will venture outside the long-only paradigm and use additional assets and strategies.

## DERIVATIVE PROFITS

A few decades ago there were trading exchanges known informally as the *commodities markets.* These exchanges were developed for farmers and commodity-related businesses. One of the difficulties with farming is that outside factors determine how much will be produced and what the market price is when it is time to sell. Weather and disease influence the quantity that is produced by both an individual farmer and the industry in general. If the weather is good and there is no outbreak of disease, the farmer is likely to have a large quantity to sell. Unfortunately, that probably means other farmers also will produce large quantities. There will be a surplus supply on the market, driving down prices. A farmer can have a record supply of product and lose money because the market price is low. Alternatively, if weather and disease work against the farmer, there will not be much product to sell. Other farmers also are likely to have low supplies, causing the market price to be high. Because the farmer has a small quantity to sell, profits might be low or nonexistent. Others in commodity-related businesses faced similar problems. Businesses that used commodities, such as food producers, could not know in advance how much they would have to pay for their raw materials or even how much would be available to buy.

The commodities exchanges provide farmers and others in the commodity-related businesses with a form of insurance. Farmers could know in advance the price they would receive for whatever quantity they produced, and users of commodities could lock in the price they would pay.

The markets provide this insurance through options and futures contracts.

A futures contract specifies an amount of the commodity that will be bought and sold at a fixed price on a fixed date. For example, before the growing season a corn farmer might agree to sell his entire output at harvest time for a set price. The farmer knows the revenue he will receive at the end of the season and can budget his expenses. The farmer takes two risks with the contract. One risk is that the growing season will be so bad that he (or she) will not produce the amount agreed to in the contract. The other risk is that market prices might be higher than the contract price; if he can produce the full contract amount, he would earn more by not entering into the futures contract. The futures contract limits the farmer's losses if the market price is low, but it also limits the potential profits if the market price is high.

The other party to the futures contract is likely to be a user of the commodity such as a food processor or a livestock farmer who uses the corn as food for livestock. The contract gives this party the advantage of knowing both the quantity that will be purchased and the price paid at harvest time. The main risk this party takes is that the market price turns out to be lower than the contract price. There also is a risk that the farmer is unable to deliver the quantity under the contract.

A futures contract obligates the buyer and seller to make the transaction on the contract date. An alternative is the option contract, which gives one party to the contract the right but not the obligation to act at the end of the contract.

For example, the corn farmer can buy a put option. This gives him the right on the option expiration date to sell the stated quantity of corn at the contract price to the option seller. The option seller has the obligation to buy the corn at the contract price if the buyer exercises the option. But the farmer does not have to exercise the option. If the market price is higher than the option price, the farmer can let the option expire and sell the corn in the market.

A commodity user can purchase a call option. This gives him the right to buy the corn at the option price. But if the market price is lower, he can let the option expire and buy the corn in the market.

Futures and options contracts are known as derivatives, because the investors are trading contract rights instead of the actual commodities. The prices of the contracts are derived from the prices of the underlying commodities.

In a simplified, textbook commodity market, the farmer and the commodity user would enter into a contract directly. But it would be cumbersome and expensive for the farmer to contact commodity users until he finds one willing to enter into a contract for the amount and price he desires. It is much more efficient for the farmer and the commodity producer to use the brokers, investors, and other middlemen of the exchange. The farmer submits his order for a contract to a broker, and the broker matches it with other orders he and other brokers have received to find a buyer.

In addition to commodity producers and users, investors enter into transactions on the commodity exchanges. There are different reasons for investors to take positions in commodities. Some simply are speculating on the future price of a commodity. They have a forecast on the direction of the price and want to profit from that forecast. Others are hedging against inflation or for other reasons want commodity-related positions in their portfolios. These investors add liquidity to the commodity exchanges and make them more efficient.

In addition to being derivatives, futures and options also are leveraged investments. They are leveraged because a relatively small amount of money can control a large amount of a commodity. A futures contract generally can be purchased for about 10 percent of the final value of the commodity in the contract. The rest of the value of the commodity almost never has to be paid. If the investor profits from the transaction, the profit is credited to his account. If the transaction is a loss, he has to pay the difference between the commodity price he bet on in the contract and the actual price of the commodity on the contract date. An option contract is purchased by paying a premium. If the investor loses money on the option, he lets the contract expire and loses the premium. With either type of contract, the investor can profit from the full price change of the commodity while putting up only a small portion of the value of the underlying commodity.

## FINANCIAL COMMODITIES

The two major commodity exchanges in the United States were the Chicago Board of Trade founded in 1848 and the Chicago Mercantile Exchange founded in 1874. The two exchanges agreed to merge in 2006. It is no coincidence that the two exchanges were founded in Chicago. The city is centralized both geographically and in relation to key transportation hubs (the Mississippi River and railways). Many farmers brought their grain and livestock to Chicago to be sold, which is why the city was once known as the "hog butcher to the world."

For many decades, the exchanges traded only farm-related commodities, such as grains, meats, orange juice, cocoa, and the like. More recently, thanks to changes in the financial markets and the insights of a few people, additional contracts were added to the exchanges and turned them into futures and options exchanges instead of commodity exchanges.

After World War II, the developed nations of the West entered into the Bretton Woods Agreement, which fixed the relative values of their currencies. As a result, there was little or no trading of currencies. In 1969, the agreement was unraveling. Leo Melamed, head of the Chicago Mercantile Exchange, concluded that the demise of fixed exchange rates would result in a trading opportunity. There would be a demand to trade and hedge currency prices, so there would be a demand for futures and options contracts involving exchanges. At the time, the exchange was shrinking, trading only meats. Melamed was looking for new contracts so the exchange could grow.

The currency futures were popular. The exchanges realized that derivative contracts did not have to be limited to physical commodities. Financial instruments could be the basis of futures and options contracts. The Chicago Merc and other exchanges began looking for other types of contracts to offer. Next up, the Chicago Board of Trade offered trading on contracts derived from bonds, especially Treasury bonds. The next major development was in 1982 when the Kansas City Board of Trade offered a futures contract based on the Value Line Stock Index. This opened a wave of financial innovation. Now, there are futures and options contracts for most stock market indexes and many subindexes. In addition, contracts for many individual stocks are traded.

With the help of academic researchers and others, the exchanges developed many innovative contracts. Large investment firms have gone a step further and developed their own contracts based on exchange-traded derivatives or by using the derivatives to hedge the positions taken in the contracts. These contracts are generically known as *synthetics*. For example, the mortgage and bond markets have developed so that an investor can do far more than purchase a mortgage or bond or even a futures position related to a bond or mortgage. Investors can purchase different parts of a bond, known as *tranches*. An investor can purchase only the stream of interest payments or only the right to principal repayment. The interest and principal payments from a pool of mortgages also are divided so that some tranches have a higher probability of being paid than others do. There also are more complicated contracts that are fully understood by a relatively few investors.

These instruments initially were developed to help businesses hedge their positions. For example, a bank that wrote a mortgage at a fixed interest rate can buy a contract to protect some of its profit if interest rates should decline and the borrower prepays the mortgage. These contracts developed into instruments known as *interest rate swaps* and *inverse floaters*. Of course, they also can be used by investors who want to invest based on their market or economic forecasts. The variety of contracts available allows the investors to be as conservative or aggressive as they desire.

The development of each derivative went through a cycle. Initially, the derivative was developed to benefit businesses, as in our earlier example of the farmers and the users of commodities. Then, investors learned they could use the derivatives to seek profits by anticipating changes in prices and investing according to the forecast. Finally, investors learned they could use the new derivatives to give them some control over how changes in the markets will affect their portfolios. This last use of derivatives is where higher mathematics merges with the investment markets and with the portfolios of both institutions and individual investors.

## THE DARK SIDE OF DERIVATIVES

Derivatives are considered highly risky and even dangerous investments by most investors. This view was developed by a couple of public events, as well as anecdotes of which everyone seems to have a version.

The first public incident involved portfolio insurance and the stock market crash of October 1987.

In the 1970s and 1980s, as derivatives markets developed beyond commodities, a couple of academic researchers developed the concept of portfolio insurance. The idea was that an investor could purchase loss insurance on a portfolio. The potential losses of an equity portfolio could be limited by the use of derivatives and a trading strategy. Portfolio insurance initially used options on individual stocks, but switched to stock index futures when those contracts were developed in the early 1980s.

The concept is simple. Its application can be quite complicated. An investor owns a stock portfolio and uses some cash to buy a futures contract that appreciates if the stock index declines. As the stock market declines, the investor sells some stocks to raise cash. This process continues as long as the market declines. After the market decline is over, stocks are purchased as it rises. With portfolio insurance the investor can decide the maximum loss he is willing to sustain in a market decline. There are costs to this, of course. The firm designing and advising on the strategy must be paid. There also is the cost of the futures contracts. Also, the insurance puts a ceiling on the gains that will be earned when stock indexes are rising. As the stock index appreciates, losses on the futures contracts plus the costs of portfolio insurance keep the portfolio from earning as much as the stock portfolio would without the insurance.

The concepts of market efficiency and liquidity underlie portfolio insurance. Market efficiency should keep a tight relationship between the value of the futures contract and the prices for which the individual stocks making up the index are selling. Liquidity requires that there be willing buyers as the insured portfolio sells stocks into the decline.

The market, however, lost its efficiency and liquidity in the market crash of October 19, 1987. The S&P 500 Index lost about 23 percent that day, but the related futures contract declined by about 29 percent. Market theory teaches that such a gap should not occur. In addition, selling was so strong on the exchanges that investors had difficulty finding buyers for stocks they were directed to sell under their portfolio insurance programs. Since the programs required selling at any price, continued selling drove prices down further, triggering more sell orders from the programs. The selling seemed to feed on itself. Despite the market anomalies, portfolio insurance apparently achieved its purposes that day by limiting losses in the portfolios, but at a cost far higher than investors expected.

Portfolio insurance is considered by many to have either caused or worsened the crash of 1987. This belief is supported by the Presidential Task Force that examined the market crash, known generally as the *Brady Report.* This report pegs portfolio insurance as a source of most of the decline, calling it "mechanical, price-insensitive selling." The negative publicity and the fact that portfolio insurance did not perform as expected in the ultimate test of the strategy drove most investors away from the concept and also gave futures and hedging bad reputations among a number of investors.

The second incident involved Orange County, California. In the early 1990s, investors still had hopes of earning high yields on their short-term investments similar to those earned in the early 1980s. But interest rates were in a decline that began in 1982 and persisted through 2006. Some investors came to believe that they could earn high yields with very low risk by using derivatives. One of those investors was the government of Orange County, California. Local governments tend to have irregular cash flow. They usually receive property tax payments once or twice a year. That gives them large cash balances that have to last the rest of the year. The cash is invested to earn some interest income. But the investments must be safe, so that no principal is lost. The investments also must be liquid. The government must be able to sell them on short notice to pay bills.

Orange County thought it had found such an investment in certain derivatives. The derivatives it selected, however, had these qualities only if interest rates did not rise. The value of the derivatives could decline quite sharply if interest rates were to rise. In 1994 interest rates did rise. The Federal Reserve caught many investors by surprise with a series of sharp rate increases. This caused Orange County's investments to lose significant value. The county eventually declared bankruptcy and sued the investment firms that advised it on the purchase of the derivatives. The incident made headlines nationwide and still forms the views of many investors regarding derivatives.

There is a key point about these two incidents that often is overlooked. In each case, the losses on the strategies were due to liquidity problems in the markets. Because of sudden, unexpected forces, investors suddenly did not want to buy these investments at any price. There was what is known as a "flight to quality." Investors wanted to own only safe government bonds. The lack of buyers caused prices to crash. But the liquidity crisis in each case was temporary. The markets recovered, investor confidence returned, and the prices recovered.

The details of the third incident are different for each investor. Most investors seem to know a friend, relative, or coworker who lost money in an options or futures investment. With options, an investor loses the entire premium paid if the option expires. For example, if the investor buys a call option, which is a bet that the investment's price will rise, the option will be worthless if the investment declines. With a futures contract, the investor can lose more than the initial investment. A futures contract usually is purchased with a cash investment equal to about 10 percent of the value of the contract. After the contract's expiration date, the losing party to the contract pays the winning party the difference between the contract price and the actual price of the underlying securities.

A number of individual investors venture into futures and options investments without a sound grounding in the potential to lose money and the ways to use derivatives effectively. They also do not understand how derivatives are priced and the importance of buying only at the right price. Because of these factors, the investors lose their entire investments or more. They sour on derivatives, and sour other investors to whom they tell their stories.

# RELATIVE RETURNS VS.
# ABSOLUTE RETURNS

Derivatives have their risks. Used properly, however, derivatives can increase the probability that an investor will achieve his or her goals. That is how they are being used in the new portfolio strategies and how they are likely to enhance portfolios in the future.

With the long-only portfolio, it is difficult for an investor to achieve true diversification. As we learned in Chapter 4, a portfolio is properly diversified only if there are assets that have little or no correlation with each other. In the traditional long-only portfolio, the investments tend to be fairly closely correlated with each other and with major economic factors such as interest rates, inflation, and economic growth. The portfolios tend to rise and fall in line with the major stock and bond indexes. Derivatives allow an investor to seek investment positions that are not correlated with long-only investments or that depend on the movements of the major economic factors and market indexes.

Another use of derivatives arises when an investor wants to reduce the risks in a portfolio without selling positions. Reducing risk without scaling back existing positions is difficult in a long-only portfolio. But the introduction of derivatives allows the investor to reduce or eliminate risks such as broad market declines. These hedging positions can be permanent, or they can be put in place only when the investor believes market risks are high. This is a form of portfolio insurance.

Derivatives also allow an investor to add leverage to a portfolio. While leverage can increase risk, it also allows the investor to increase the potential return and to decrease risk by creating a portfolio with true diversification. Remember that a portfolio of risky assets actually is less risky than any of the individual assets if the investments have negative correlations with each other.

Leverage greatly increases the opportunities open to an investor. For example, the bulk of the portfolio can be invested in risk-free or low-risk assets that also will have low returns. The remainder of the portfolio can be invested in a variety of risky assets. Purchasing these assets with derivatives means only a small amount of cash is needed, and the potential gains are magnified far beyond the returns possible with a nonleveraged, long-only purchase. This type of positioning often is known as a *barbell strategy*.

The key difference between a portfolio with derivatives and one without derivatives is in the concept of relative returns versus absolute returns.

Relative returns are the returns of an investment manager or investment vehicle compared to a market index or benchmark. For example, most mutual funds that invest in U.S. stocks are compared to the Standard & Poor's 500 Index. If the fund earns a higher return than the index, the manager is considered to be good or skillful. This means that in a declining market, an investor can make a good investment decision that loses a lot of money. If the index declines 25 percent and the mutual fund loses only 20 percent of its value, the fund is considered a big winner. The investor has earned great returns relative to the index but has earned poor returns on an absolute basis.

An absolute return investment is one that is not measured against a broad index and whose return pattern tends to be independent of the index. Absolute return investments also tend to earn positive returns over time that do not depend on a particular direction of inflation, interest rates, economic growth, or the major market indexes. A grouping of relative return investments can be an absolute return portfolio if the investments are uncorrelated with each other. For example, a simple two-asset portfolio could consist of a stock index fund and a derivative investment that sells short the index. These assets should have a negative correlation and jointly would be an absolute return portfolio.

Absolute returns are critical to long-term investment success because, as we have seen, the major market indexes can endure long periods of negative or low returns. The individual investor is not served well by the traditional relative-return portfolio during such periods. During bull markets, a diversified portfolio that seeks absolute returns will earn lower returns than a traditional long-only portfolio. But the absolute return portfolio should have less risk and volatility than the long-only portfolio, should earn similar returns to the long-only portfolio over the long-term, and will earn higher returns during the extended periods when the long-only portfolio is earning less than its long-term average.

## PORTFOLIOS OF THE FUTURE

The tools and strategies of the portfolios of the future are already available and are being used by some investors. Endowments and foundations usually lead the way to innovative investment strategies. Unlike pension funds, these organizations generally are not subject to public scrutiny of their investment decisions and do not face short-term performance pressure. They can try new techniques. The low profile also gives endowments and foundations access to resources and strategies not usually available to individual investors, as does the amount of money they have to invest. They can also take a long-term perspective since the funds are supposed to last forever. Yet the investment pools of endowments and foundations are supposed to pay income to their sponsoring organizations each year. The need to pay income and to make the portfolio last for an extended period is similar to the goals of many individual investors.

In general, endowments and foundations switched from relative-return investing to absolute-return investing some time ago and have had good experiences with this approach. These investors also have been among the first users of derivatives for something other than speculation. The strategies used by endowments and foundations are making their way into the portfolios of individual investors.

Individual investors have more tools and information available to them. New or recent innovations in financial instruments we have discussed include options, index funds, futures contracts for equities and equity indexes, and leveraged investments. Individual investors also can use inverse investments. These are derivatives that generate positive returns when the underlying investments decline.

As we have discussed, derivatives and absolute return investments provide several positive benefits. They can increase returns, especially during periods when long-only investments are performing poorly. Perhaps more importantly, these tools allow an investor to control risks. The investor can create a properly diversified portfolio instead of being limited to the less effective diversification of a long-only portfolio. The leverage of derivatives also enables the investor to control risk levels. Derivatives and leverage enable the investor to customize exposure to different risks and sources of potential return.

Technology and financial innovation give investors direct and relatively inexpensive access to these benefits. Computers, databases, and the Internet make available past returns from these different instruments and allow the construction of hypothetical portfolios. The investor also can see current performance of the different vehicles and can determine the values and relative values of different investments. Financial services companies also are making these tools available to individual investors through mutual funds, exchange-traded funds, funds of funds, and other means. Just a few years ago, all of these benefits were available only to the wealthiest and most sophisticated investors or were very expensive to access.

There are many ways investors can use derivatives and absolute return investing to increase returns and control risk. For example, an investor can create what is known as a long-short equity portfolio. In this portfolio, the investor purchases stocks that are attractive and sells short stocks that are unattractive. There are several ways to construct long-short portfolios, including using leverage to increase exposure to the markets beyond the level possible with all-cash investments.

Despite the many advantages of derivatives and long-short investing, few individual investors should attempt these strategies on their own. Even endowments and foundations that use these strategies tend to hire outside investment firms to develop and implement the strategies; the endowments employ staff to oversee these outside managers. Or the endowment will implement the strategies itself, but it will hire staff members to work full time on each strategy. The anecdotes of individual investors losing money using derivatives occur because the individuals generally implement the strategies on their own.

Instead, individual investors should rely on financial service firms and money managers to implement the strategies. The investors should decide which absolute return strategies and which derivatives are appropriate for them, and then select the financial professionals to implement them. Because of innovations in recent years, many of the strategies available to endowments and other large investors also are available to individual investor at reasonable cost. Individuals do not have access to all of the vehicles available to endowments, but versions of many of them are available. We reviewed some of them in Chapter 6, especially in the section on hedge fund investing through mutual funds. We look at more of the portfolio strategies in this section. Many of these currently are available to most investors, but a few are not. I expect that all of these and more will be available to most investors in the near future.

## Long-Short Portfolios

The *long-short portfolio* is the classic hedge fund and absolute return strategy. There are different ways of creating long-short portfolios—and they can be created with or without derivatives.

The initial idea of a hedge fund was to actually hedge a stock portfolio against a potential market decline. To do this, the hedge fund purchases stocks the manager believes have the potential to appreciate and sells short stocks the manager believes are likely to decline. In one variation, known as a market-neutral strategy, the long and short positions tend to be equal. Market-neutral portfolios often have a rate of return goal similar to that of short-term Treasury bonds or a little higher. Other long-short funds take predominantly long positions with short positions often being 20 percent to 30 percent of the portfolio. The goal of some of these funds often is to earn an alpha above the stock market index rather than a positive return most of the time. Others believe that their decisions will be sufficiently accurate to generate a positive return most years, even when the stock market indexes sharply decline.

For example, *Schwab Hedged Equity* uses a quantitative stock ranking system developed by Schwab's staff. The fund purchases stocks that are rated A or B by the system. It sells short stocks rated D or F. The fund tries to control the positions so that there is not excessive exposure to industry sectors relative to the index. The short positions range from 20 percent to 60 percent of the portfolio.

A different strategy is used by the *Calamos Market Neutral Income* fund. This fund buys convertible securities. These generally are corporate bonds that can be converted into stock at a future point for a stated price per share. Convertible bonds pay higher yields than stocks but lower yields than bonds. The fund generally sells short the stocks underlying the convertible securities and might also use options to hedge its convertible positions. The goal of the fund is to earn annual returns of 8 percent to 10 percent regardless of market index returns.

A growing form of the long-short fund uses leverage to purchase some or all of the stocks in the long part of the portfolio. Initially, these were known as 120/20 portfolios. They were long 120 percent of the portfolio because of leverage and short 20 percent. More recently the most common form of the strategy is 130/30, though some fund managers are offering 170/70 long-short portfolios.

These are just a few examples of different long-short strategies, and they are two that are available through mutual funds to individual investors.

## Portable Alpha

One of the most frequently used and fastest-growing derivative strategies is *portable alpha*. Recall that investment returns can be divided into two portions: beta and alpha. Beta is the return from the broad asset class or index. If a mutual fund has a beta of 1.0 to the Standard & Poor's 500 Index, its returns are determined entirely by the index. When the index rises 5 percent, the fund will rise 5 percent. When the index declines 5 percent, the fund will decline 5 percent. Alpha is the return that is independent of the index or benchmark and generally is considered to be a measure of a manager's skill when the investment is a mutual fund or investment account.

To use portable alpha, the investor first determines the asset allocation he wants for the portfolio. Suppose 40 percent of the portfolio is allocated to the S&P 500. The investor would like to earn a return above the index with that part of the portfolio. He or she searches available mutual funds but does not have confidence that any of them is consistently able to earn an alpha above the index. However, there are money managers in other asset classes or segments of the market in whom the investor has confidence. Some appear able to earn alpha above their benchmarks. Others use absolute return strategies that will earn a consistent positive return.

The investor can take a small portion of the cash he or she has allocated for the S&P 500 position and use that to buy derivatives that generate the beta of the index. The investor can buy futures or options or even contract with a large financial services firm. This position might use 5 percent to 10 percent of the cash though it can use 20 percent of the cash or more.

The remaining cash can be invested with one of the other managers. For example, the investor can invest it all with an absolute return manager. If that manager earns a consistent return of 3 percent annually, the investor will earn the S&P 500 return plus three percentage points. (This example ignores the costs of the derivative position. One cost is the transaction cost of buying the derivative. In addition, there is a financing cost of owning the derivative since the investor puts down only 10 percent of the value of the index exposure. The financing cost usually is the LIBOR (London Interbank Offered Rate) interest rate on the full index exposure. That means for portable alpha to break even, the portable alpha manager must earn at a minimum the transaction cost plus the LIBOR rate on the derivative position.)

Alternatively, the investor can invest the remaining cash with a manager who earns a consistent alpha above a benchmark other than the S&P 500. That decision results in a more complicated strategy. Suppose the superior manager invests in U.S. small-capitalization stocks. The investor does not want the additional beta of small stocks in this portion of the portfolio. He or she gives most of the cash to the small stock manager, but with a portion of it the investor eliminates the small stock beta by selling short a small stock index using futures or options. The net effect of those two transactions, after expenses, is that the short position and the beta of the small stock manager offset each other. All that remains is the alpha earned by the small stock manager.

Some mutual funds already use these or similar strategies. Consider *PIMCO Commodity Real Return* and other commodity mutual funds that take comparable approaches. The PIMCO fund uses a portion of fund assets to buy contracts that promise to pay the fund the return of a published commodity index. The contracts are with major financial services firms that are financially secure. With the rest of the fund's assets, PIMCO invests in bonds, an asset class in which PIMCO has expertise. Investors earn the return of the commodity index and have its beta, which has a low or negative correlation to U.S. stocks. In addition, the investor earns whatever return PIMCO is able to generate from the bonds. In times of rising interest rates, that portion of the fund is likely to have a negative return. At other times, it is likely to generate a positive return, and with PIMCO's record it is likely to be a return above that of the bond index.

It is likely that over time PIMCO and other mutual fund families will use this and similar strategies in many of their mutual funds. Historically, a fund company begins with one or two funds and develops a reputation in that asset class. It then either remains a small boutique fund group or adds funds in other asset classes to be a full-service family. It is rare that one of the broader based companies is considered to have consistent skill levels across the asset classes. With portable alpha, the fund group can give investors diversification without finding skill in other asset classes by using portable alpha.

Fund groups might take an additional step by offering funds of only alpha strategies with betas independent of major market indexes. Such funds already are being offered to institutional investors. Here is an example of how such funds compare with traditional mutual funds. Suppose in its Total Return bond fund, PIMCO anticipates that mortgages will perform better than Treasury bonds in the coming year and positions the portfolio accordingly. Over the next year, the forecast turns out to be correct, but both mortgages and Treasury bonds have negative returns. The fund earns an alpha over the bond market index because it correctly forecast the different relative returns in mortgages and treasuries, but it has a negative return because both investments declined. In an alpha strategy fund,

PIMCO would take the same positions, and then use derivatives to offset most of the decline in mortgages and Treasury bonds. Investors in this fund would earn the alpha but avoid the negative return generated by the beta of the bond index. PIMCO offers such a fund to institutional investors.

The investor should bear in mind the full costs of a portable alpha strategy. The main cost is financing rate of a futures contract on an index position, as mentioned earlier. This rate usually is the "interest rate on risk-free cash," which most often is the LIBOR interest rate. In early 2007, that was 5 percent to 5.25 percent. The financing rate is subtracted from the return of the index replicated by the futures contract to determine the net return to the investor from the derivative position. At a minimum, the return earned by the portable alpha manager must exceed this cost. In addition, since the portable alpha manager is working with less than 100 percent of the cash allocated to that portion of the portfolio (the rest being invested in the futures contract), the rate of return earned by that manager must exceed the risk-free rate. Only the return earned by the portfolio manager that exceeds the costs will be alpha to the total portfolio.

Portable alpha allows the investor to target the amount of risk he or she is willing to take by establishing the beta of the portfolio. It also allows for earning the highest return possible by seeking alpha wherever the investor finds it. In addition, with portable alpha an investor does not have to limit the amount of money given to a quality manager simply because the investor already is fully exposed to that manager's asset class.

## Structured Investments

This category includes an array of investments that essentially are contracts between an investor and a financial services firm, usually an insurer or large brokerage firm. The products usually become more popular when the stock market indexes are in decline. They also are drawing more interest as the Baby Boomers age and become more interested in safety and income and less interested in maximizing long-term growth.

One common structured investment, perhaps the most popular, is known generically as an *equity index annuity* (EIA).

An equity indexed annuity starts with two simple, attractive notions. The returns of the annuity are tied by a formula to a stock market index instead of to interest rates. In addition, unlike the stock market the EIAs offer bear market protection. Most EIAs guarantee that the account will not decline in value, and a few have modest minimum return guarantees of 1 percent to 3 percent. The EIA essentially is a hybrid of variable annuities and fixed annuities. Like the variable annuity, returns can be higher than current interest rates when the stock market does well. Like the fixed annuity, returns won't be negative when the stock indexes decline. As with all annuities, the EIA's earnings are tax deferred until distributed.

Each insurer has its own formulas for determining the returns credited to an investor's account. This book is not the place for a detailed examination of these formulas and their differences. The investor should know, nevertheless, that the EIA will not receive the full return of the index, and the formula used should be examined closely. The formulas can be difficult to understand. It is best to review examples of the returns that were or would be credited to the account in each of the last few calendar years. In addition to the limits imposed by the formulas, the EIAs usually have a maximum return of 7 percent to 10 percent annually. Even if the stock index has a significantly higher return and the formula gives a higher return to the investor, the investor will not participate above the ceiling.

There are a range of structured investments that are very similar to the EIA, though without the tax deferral of an annuity. Some of the investments are very simple, based on straightforward factors such as changes in interest rates or stock indexes. Others are much more complicated. In all these products, the investor generally is guaranteed at least that the initial investment will be returned after a period of time, usually 10 years. There is the potential for a return exceeding those of safe investments such as certificates of deposit and Treasury notes, if the stock index or other benchmark performs well.

An investor might want to review how an investment firm can make such promises and consider constructing a portfolio to achieve similar results and save the fees. The firms generally use most of the investor's money to buy an investment such as a zero-coupon bond. This is an instrument that does not pay interest but sells at a discount to its face value. At maturity, it pays the face value. For example, an investor deposits $100,000 in an account. The financial services firm agrees at a minimum to return that amount in 10 years. The firm purchases a zero-coupon bond that will pay $100,000 in 10 years; let us say the bond costs $70,000 today. With the remaining $30,000 (ignoring costs), the firm purchases futures on a stock index, a stock index fund, or another investment. The gains from that investment are used to pay whatever gains are credited to the investor's account, and the firm keeps any additional gains.

In lieu of purchasing a structured investment, the investor can use the money to create a structured investment in his or her own portfolio similar to the one just described. The investor can purchase a zero-coupon Treasury bond that guarantees a return of the principal amount in 10 years, and invest the rest of the money in an appropriate vehicle. The benefits of some structured investments cannot be replicated easily or in a cost-effective way by most individual investors. Before purchasing such investments, however, the investor should consider if the same or similar results can be obtained at lower cost by combining readily available investments.

An appeal of structured products is that they can be customized to the investor's needs, at least if the investor has enough money to invest. But they also are illiquid; the investor is unlikely to be able to sell them to another investor, and the contract terms allow an early exit only with payment of a penalty. The contracts also make it difficult for an investor to compare alternatives and to determine all the fees charged.

## Innovative Mutual Funds

Most individual investors are wary of investing directly in derivatives, and they probably should be. To reach one's goals, an investor needs to know a lot about futures and options before investing in them. Investing without this prior knowledge is the reason so many investors know anecdotes of investors who lost all or even more of their investments in futures or options. The prices of these contracts vary based on the time until maturity of the contract, interest rates, the volatility of the underlying investment, the price of the underlying investment, the market's forecast of the direction of the underlying investment, and probably other factors. Hedging a portfolio or looking to profit from a big move in an investment is not as simple as telling a broker to buy futures or options. The investor must decide which contract to buy, the quantity of the contract, and the appropriate price to pay for it.

A couple of innovative mutual fund groups have developed funds that give investors access to some of the benefits of derivatives without requiring investors to know the details of how to trade in those contracts. These fund groups are Rydex and ProFunds, and there are others vying for this market.

For example, Rydex has a series of funds it calls *Dynamic* while ProFunds has counterparts called *Ultra*. These funds use futures and options to try to achieve a return equal to 200 percent of the return of a stated market index. (The funds actually will not earn double the return of the index because of the costs of the futures contracts as discussed in the Portable Alpha section of this chapter. The higher short-term interest rates are, the greater the return will be from its target.) There also are *Inverse* funds at each group that bet against, or sell short, market benchmarks. Some of these try to only get the inverse of the index return; if the index earns a positive 5 percent, the fund should earn a negative 5 percent. Others seek to double the inverse of the index return. If the index earns a positive 5 percent, these funds will earn a negative 10 percent.

These different types of funds cover more than the major stock market indexes. There now are such funds investing in international stocks and emerging market stocks and the dollar. There also are leveraged and inverse funds based on interest rate changes. Rydex offers funds that combine several of these funds or uses other investments to build absolute-return or hedge fund–like portfolios.

Investors can use these funds in lieu of direct derivative investments in some of the ways already discussed. If an investor believes strongly that an investment is likely to move in a certain direction (either up or down), a leveraged fund can be purchased to amplify the index return. Or if the investor wants to hedge a portfolio position, this can be done with an inverse fund or half as much cash can be used by purchasing a leveraged inverse fund. The inverse funds allow an investor to construct a portfolio that is not a long-only portfolio, so a portion of the portfolio will be rising when the conventional stock and bond indexes are declining. The major difference between these funds and direct investments in derivatives is that the leverage is not as great. With a direct purchase of a futures contract, the investors can put down only 10 percent or so of the contract value. But with the funds, the investor invests 100 percent of the cash. The leverage is within the fund. The fund also charges management fees.

Each fund group offers education materials on its web site to help an investor better understand the derivatives in the funds and different ways the funds can be used.

# Hedged Mutual Funds

As discussed in Chapter 6, a few mutual funds are available that use traditional hedge fund or absolute return strategies. One such fund is Hussman Strategic Growth. It uses both traditional long investments in stocks and derivatives to either hedge or leverage those positions.

Hussman first uses its own model to select a portfolio of primarily U.S. stocks. The fund usually owns approximately 200 stocks; and the model identifies stocks selling at valuations that are low relative to the growth rates of the companies. The fund also has models and indicators that examine the valuation of the market and what it calls the *market climate*, which essentially are market trends and investor confidence.

If the models indicate that stocks generally are overvalued and the climate is negative, the fund will use derivatives (primarily options) to hedge the portfolio. The amount of hedging depends on how negative the valuation and climate readings are. If both major factors are negative, the portfolio of stocks might be completely hedged. In that case, if the indexes decline the derivatives could generate enough profits to offset losses in the fund's stocks. In addition, if the stocks perform better than the indexes, the fund could have gains while the markets overall are declining. Another possibility is that the stocks in the portfolio earn positive returns though the indexes earn negative returns, and the derivatives also are profitable. Through these strategies the fund generated positive returns in the bear market years of 2001 and 2002. The fund returned over 14 percent each year. The hedging can reduce returns if the indexes earn positive returns. This happened in 2003, 2004, and 2006. This experience shows the results of using an absolute return strategy. Such strategies have better results than long-only indexes in bad times but can earn lower (though still positive) returns when the indexes do well.

Likewise, if the indicators show that stocks are undervalued and market climate is positive, derivatives will be used to leverage the stock portfolio. The fund will earn more than the indexes if the indexes have positive returns, perhaps considerably more than the indexes depending on the amount of leverage used and how well the stocks in the portfolio perform. If the market indexes decline, however, despite the favorable indicators, the fund is likely to decline more than the indexes.

There are only a few mutual funds using such strategies. Institutional investors can choose from a number of firms offering such strategies and also more sophisticated ones. Two leaders in this field are Bridgewater Associates and Barclays Global Investors.

In 2006, Bridgewater told clients that it would cease accepting traditional actively managed strategies and offer only its Pure Alpha and All Weather strategies. With Pure Alpha the firm uses its "best ideas" from its range of active investment strategies. The positions in this strategy tend to make significant use of derivatives and hedging. For example, the firm might conclude that the dollar is likely to decline relative to the Japanese yen. In response it would purchase futures in the yen. The strategy could have 30 or more such positions at one time, covering stocks and bonds around the globe plus interest rates, currencies, and commodities. In addition, Bridgewater says it can customize the strategy to meet the risk level desired by the investor. It can add or subtract asset classes and adjust the amount of leverage.

Barclay's has a similar strategy called *Global Ascent.* Its methods for determining the investment positions are different than Bridgewater's, so the array of positions usually is different. This strategy is also filled with positions using derivatives and hedging strategies similar to Bridgewater's. Global Ascent also covers the range of investment opportunities available worldwide.

A number of traditional hedge funds seek opportunities similar to those in these Bridgewater and Barclays' offerings. Few are able to invest in the breadth of positions available through these strategies. Such offerings are not yet available to individual investors through mutual funds. I believe it is only a matter of time before a few funds composed of pure alpha strategies primarily using derivatives are offered to retail investors.

In previous chapters we learned that investors need to be forward-looking when analyzing the markets and determining the positions to place in their portfolios. They also need to be forward-looking in considering the investment vehicles and strategies they will use. In addition to the traditional long-only investments, derivatives and hedging strategies are available. These and other tools are more accessible to individual investors than they were a few years ago, and more innovations are likely. The investor who learns when it is appropriate to use such tools and how to take advantage of them can increase returns, control risk, improve diversification, and better control the volatility of the portfolio.

In coming years, the foxlike investor will develop a portfolio with certain characteristics:

- There will be investments in addition to traditional long-only investments.
- Risk reduction will be as important as potential returns.
- Relative return investing, in which investors seek to match or beat the return of a major market index, will be supplemented or replaced by absolute return investing in which investors seek consistent positive returns that are independent of major market indexes and major economic forces.
- True diversification will exist by including derivatives and investments that have low or negative correlation with traditional market indexes.
- One or more managers in the portfolio will seek to maximize alpha while minimizing or eliminating the beta of a traditional long-only index.

- One or more managers in the portfolio will eschew long-only investments entirely and use derivatives to seek only alpha with little or no correlation to long-only indexes.
- Managers with superior alpha-generating abilities will be paired with derivatives so that the alpha can be maximized without changing the portfolio's beta.
- The risk and volatility of a portfolio will be controlled or reduced through the use of derivatives, inverse investments, nontraditional managers and other means.
- Costs for any quality other than top performance will decline. Derivatives, exchange-traded funds and other vehicles make earning beta in most other assets very inexpensive. Money managers will be paid only for consistent alpha and risk reduction.
- The investor will increasingly focus on the portfolio as a whole and how the pieces of the portfolio work together and focus less on analyzing individual investments in the portfolio.

# Index